LITERATU[...] FOR ENGLISH

BEGINNING

Burton Goodman

Series Editor: Anne Petti Smith
Executive Editor: Linda Kwil
Creative Director: Michael E. Kelly
Marketing Manager: Thomas Dare
Production Manager: Genevieve Kelley

Send all inquiries to:

McGraw-Hill/Contemporary
One Prudential Plaza
130 E. Randolph Ave. Suite 400
Chicago, IL 60601

ISBN: 0-07-256530-6

Printed in the United States of America.

1 2 3 4 5 6 7 8 9 10 QPD 08 07 06 05 04 03 02

The McGraw·Hill Companies

Contents

Acknowledgments

Retellings and/or adaptations of "Wolf" by Jack London, "Crucita" by Manuela Williams Crosno, "The Last Leaf" by O. Henry, "The Hero" by Stephen Crane, "Land" by Leo Tolstoy, and "Mrs. Penn's Story" by Mary Wilkins Freeman are by Burton Gordon.

"Crucita" (originally titled "Crucita's Image") © 1987 by Manuela Williams Crosno. Adapted and reprinted by permission of the author's agent, Burton Goodman.

To the Teacher

About the *Literature for English* Program

Literature for English is a literature-based skills program designed to help readers improve their basic English skills.

Each book in the series contains outstanding stories by famous writers. The language in the stories is controlled so that they can be easily understood by students. Depending on the level, the stories are divided into a number of short, illustrated sections to assist the reader in understanding the selection. Many of the chapters in the Advanced Levels contain theme-related stories and poems.

A pre-reading section entitled **GETTING READY TO READ** introduces each story in this book. The component parts, **The Story and You, Learning About Literature,** and **Looking Ahead,** provide high-interest material to motivate the learner to read the story that follows. This section also offers important information about elements of literature.

Each story is followed by a comprehensive four-part skills check that is specially developed to meet the needs of LEP readers and is consistent with the general scope and sequence for ESL curricula.

The skills check provides a wide variety of hands-on practice in reading, writing, speaking, and listening. It includes the following exercises:

CHECK YOUR READING Ten self-scoring multiple-choice questions review reading comprehension, vocabulary, and idioms in the story just read. A Score Chart at the end of the book enables readers to enter their scores and see their results.

UNDERSTANDING THE STORY Varied exercises use directed writing activities for mastery of reading comprehension, sentence structure, verbs, parts of speech, writing, and punctuation. Hints to help the reader improve spelling and grammar are offered throughout.

STUDYING THE STORY Post-reading activities provide opportunities for students to work together to improve their listening, speaking, and writing skills. Specific as well as open-ended writing assignments and exercises appear in the sections **Studying the Story** and in the final section, **THINKING ABOUT LITERATURE**. Readers also complete a graphic organizer for each selection.

Literary elements explored in this series include character, plot, setting, conflict, and theme, as well as genre, such as the folktale, science fiction, and autobiography. In addition, this book contains features designed to teach and reinforce critical reading skills, such as making predictions, drawing conclusions, and reaching a decision by making inferences.

The vocabulary for each book in the series is drawn primarily from core word lists for beginning, intermediate, and advanced level students. Skills development is progressive, although it is possible to alter the sequence for intermediate and advanced level readers.

It should be noted that the Beginning book and Intermediate books use line reference numbers in the margins of the stories. These are extremely useful not only in helping the reader locate specific answers, but also in providing easy reference for reinforcement and review. The Beginning and Intermediate books also contain certain words and phrases printed in **boldfaced** type. This identifies the vocabulary and idioms that readers are tested on in the multiple-choice section following each chapter.

The Teacher's Guide provides the Answer Key for scoring **CHECK YOUR READING**, as well as suggested answers for the exercises in **UNDERSTANDING THE STORY**. At the back of the book is a list of Irregular Verbs, including their present tenses, past tenses, and past participles.

I appreciate the contributions of the many teachers, students, administrators, and ESL coordinators who offered assistance in the development of the *Literature for English* series. For their valuable suggestions, I am grateful.

The program's fine literature, attractive format, and positive approach should encourage the reader to enjoy literature and to improve their English.

Burton Goodman

Scope & Sequence

Story	Literary Elements	Grammar Structures
Unit 1: Wolf *page 1*	■ plot	■ present and past tense of verb *to be* ■ present tense of verb *to have* ■ present and past tense (regular and irregular verbs) ■ changing statements to questions ■ using adjectives ■ using pronouns
Unit 2: Crucita *page 51*	■ characterization ■ main character	■ past tense (irregular verbs) ■ using pronouns ■ using adjectives ■ changing statements to questions
Unit 3: The Last Leaf *page 91*	■ surprise ending	■ changing statements to questions ■ past tense (irregular verbs) ■ using adjectives ■ using adverbs ■ using prepositions
Unit 4: The Hero *page 133*	■ setting ■ plot	■ past tense (irregular verbs) ■ using prepositions ■ future tense with *will* ■ changing adjectives to adverbs ■ changing statements to questions
Unit 5: Land *page 161*	■ motive	■ past tense (regular and irregular verbs) ■ using pronouns ■ changing statements to questions
Unit 6: Mrs. Penn's Story *page 191*	■ conflict ■ character development	■ using adjectives and adverbs ■ past tense (irregular verbs) ■ changing statements to questions

UNIT 1
WOLF

BY JACK LONDON

GETTING READY TO READ

1. The Story and You

In "Wolf," you will meet Madge and Walt. They find a lost dog. They want to keep it as a pet. Do you have a pet? If you do, tell about your pet. What do you like about your pet? How are pets sometimes a problem?

2. Learning About Literature

The **plot** tells the important things that happen in a story. In "Wolf," Madge and Walt find a lost dog. That is the *first* thing that happens in the plot. Other things take place, or happen, in the story. The last thing that happens in the story is the *last* thing in the plot.

3. Looking Ahead

Look at the picture on the left. How many people do you see? Which people do you think live in the house? Do you think that the dog in the picture is friendly? Read on to see if you are right.

WOLF

BY JACK LONDON

PART 1

This story is about a man, a woman, and a dog. The man's name was Walt. The woman's name was Madge. The dog's name was Wolf.

Madge and Walt were married. They lived in California. They lived in a small house on top of a hill.

One night while Madge and Walt were sleeping, there suddenly was a loud sound. The sound woke them up.

"What was that?" asked Walt.

"I don't know," said Madge. "Let's look outside."

They opened the door. They looked around. "Do you see anything?" asked Madge.

"No," said Walt.

Suddenly Madge said, "Look over there!"

On the grass they saw a large, brown dog. The dog looked tired and hungry. It was lost.

Walt and Madge walked toward the dog. The dog **growled** at them. It was not a friendly dog.

"The dog is hungry," said Madge. "Let's give it some bread and milk."

They went back to the house and got the food. They put the food on the ground. The dog did not want to eat the food while they were there.

"Let's go back to the house," said Walt.

They went back to the house and looked out the window.

The dog began to eat. The dog was **starved**. It ate all the food very quickly.

"That dog eats like a wolf," said Walt.

"It looks like a wolf, too," said Madge. "Let's call him 'Wolf.'"

The next morning they **fed** Wolf again. This time the dog was a little more friendly. It let them come closer.

In the afternoon their neighbor, Mrs. Johnson, **dropped in**.

She saw Wolf. She said to Madge and Walt, "I didn't know you had a dog."

"We didn't," said Madge. "We found this dog last night. It was outside the house."

Mrs. Johnson was surprised. "Where did this dog come from?" she asked.

"We don't know," said Walt. "It was lost. It came here."

Mrs. Johnson said, "My brother, Skiff, lives in Alaska. I visited him there last year. This dog looks like the dogs I saw in Alaska. It looks like the big dogs that pull sleds there."

Madge and Walt looked at each other. They were surprised. Madge said, "But how could Wolf get here all the way from Alaska?"

Check Your Reading

Put an **X** in the box next to the correct answer.

How many questions did you answer correctly? Circle your score. Then fill in your score on the Score Chart on page 216.

Number Correct	Score
1	10
2	20
3	30
4	40
5	50
6	60
7	70
8	80
9	90
10	100

Reading Comprehension

1. Madge and Walt lived in
   - ☐ **a.** California.
   - ☐ **b.** Alaska.
   - ☐ **c.** Texas.

2. Their house was
   - ☐ **a.** on top of a hill.
   - ☐ **b.** on a busy street.
   - ☐ **c.** near some tall trees.

3. Madge and Walt woke up because they heard
   - ☐ **a.** a radio.
   - ☐ **b.** someone calling.
   - ☐ **c.** a loud sound.

4. Madge and Walt saw a large, brown
   - ☐ **a.** wolf.
   - ☐ **b.** dog.
   - ☐ **c.** sled.

5. The dog was
   - ☐ **a.** lost.
   - ☐ **b.** small.
   - ☐ **c.** happy.

6. Mrs. Johnson said that Wolf looked like
   - ☐ **a.** her dog.
   - ☐ **b.** her brother's dog.
   - ☐ **c.** dogs she saw in Alaska.

Vocabulary

7. The dog ate all the food quickly. The dog was starved. The word *starved* means
   - ☐ **a.** very hungry.
   - ☐ **b.** very sick.
   - ☐ **c.** very smart.

8. The dog was not friendly. It growled. When it *growled*, it
   - ☐ **a.** smiled.
   - ☐ **b.** made a noise.
   - ☐ **c.** sat down.

9. Madge and Walt fed Wolf again the next morning. The word *fed* means
   - ☐ **a.** yelled at.
   - ☐ **b.** hit.
   - ☐ **c.** gave food to.

Idioms

10. Their neighbor, Mrs. Johnson, dropped in. The idiom *drop in* means
    - ☐ **a.** fell down.
    - ☐ **b.** visited.
    - ☐ **c.** hurt yourself.

Understanding the Story

Exercise A ~ Checking Comprehension

Answer each question by writing a complete sentence. Begin each sentence with a capital letter, and end each sentence with a period. You may use the line numbers in parentheses to help you. The first sentence has been done for you.

1. What was the man's name? (2)

   The man's name was Walt.

2. What was the woman's name? (2)

3. What was the dog's name? (3)

4. Where did Madge and Walt live? (4)

5. What woke up Madge and Walt? (7)

6. What did they see on the grass? (14)

7. What did they give the dog? (18)

8. How much food did the dog eat? (25)

9. Where does Mrs. Johnson's brother live? (39)

10. When did Mrs. Johnson visit her brother? (40)

Exercise B ~ Building Sentences

Make sentences by adding the correct letter. The first sentence has been done for you.

1. b	Madge and Walt	a. in California.
2. ____	They lived	b. were married.
3. ____	A loud sound	c. toward the dog.
4. ____	They walked	d. woke them up.

Now do questions 5–8 the same way.

5. ____	The dog	a. some bread and milk.
6. ____	They gave it	b. fed Wolf again.
7. ____	Madge and Walt looked	c. was not friendly.
8. ____	The next morning they	d. out the window.

Now write the sentences on the lines below. Remember to begin each sentence with a capital letter and to end each sentence with a period.

1. ____________________

2. ____________________

3. ____________________

4. ____________________

5. ____________________

6. ____________________

7. ____________________

8. ____________________

____

Exercise C ~ Adding Vocabulary

In the box are 8 words from the story. Complete each sentence by adding the correct word.

dog	neighbor	married	ground
sleds	door	night	food

1. Madge and Walt were ________________.
2. They woke up during the ________________.
3. They opened the ________________.
4. On the grass they saw a ________________.
5. They put some food on the ________________.
6. The dog did not eat the ________________.
7. Mrs. Johnson was their ________________.
8. In Alaska dogs pull ________________.

Exercise D ~ Using Verbs Correctly

Fill in each blank using the **present tense** of the verb *to be (am, are, is)*. The first one has been done for you.

The present tense of the verb *to be* does not follow the usual rules. Look at the chart below. It shows the right way to write the verb.

Singular	**Plural**
[one]	[more than one]
I am	we are
you are	you are
he/she/it is	they are

This story ___is___ (1) about a man, a woman, and a dog. The man and the woman ________ (2) married. They live in a small house. It ________ (3) on top of a hill.

One night they hear a loud sound. They ________ (4) surprised. "What ________ (5) that?" asks the man. I ________ (6) not sure," says the woman. They see a dog. It ________ (7) hungry and tired.

Exercise E ~ Changing Statements to Questions

Change each statement to a question that begins with *Was* or *Were*. Put a question mark at the end of each question. The first one has been done for you.

1. The dog was tired.

   Was the dog tired?

2. The dog was hungry.

3. The dog was lost.

4. The dog was outside the house.

5. Madge and Walt were married.

6. The dog was a little more friendly.

7. Madge and Walt were sleeping.

8. Mrs. Johnson was surprised.

9. Mrs. Johnson's brother was in Alaska.

10. Madge and Walt were surprised, too.

Exercise F ~ Vocabulary Review

Part A

Write a complete sentence for each word or idiom.

1. married ______________________________

____

2. sled ______________________________

____

3. neighbor ______________________________

____

4. starved ______________________________

____

5. growled ______________________________

____

6. fed ______________________________

____

7. dropped in (idiom) ______________________________

____

Part B

Write about what happened in the story. Use three or more of the vocabulary words from Part A.

Before You Read Part 2

At the end of Part 1, Mrs. Johnson said, "This dog looks like the dogs I saw in Alaska." She said that her brother, Skiff, lives in Alaska. Do you think that Madge and Walt will ever meet Skiff? See if you are right.

PART 2

Madge and Walt fed Wolf every day. They **took long walks** with him. They liked to play with Wolf. Wolf still was not too friendly.

One afternoon Madge came out of the house. She walked down the steps and looked around. She saw Walt. He had a hammer in his hand. He was fixing the fence.

"Where is Wolf?" she asked.

"I don't know," Walt answered. "He was here a minute ago. Maybe he ran after a rabbit."

"I don't see him now," said Madge. "Here, Wolf," she called.

They walked down the road and through the tall grass.

"There he is!" said Walt. He pointed ahead.

Wolf was sitting on top of a large rock. The dog was watching them.

"Good dog," shouted Walt. "Come here."

The dog opened his mouth. He looked at Madge and Walt and ran toward them. He stopped about twenty feet away.

Madge and Walt continued to walk. Wolf ran into the tall grass. Soon they did not see him.

"Wolf will **catch up** with us later," said Madge.

Suddenly they heard something. The sound was coming from the woods. They saw a man. He came out of the woods and walked toward them.

Madge and Walt did not know the man. He was very tall, and he looked very strong. He had wide shoulders. He had long hair and a thick, black beard. He was holding his hat in his hand.

"Good afternoon," said Walt. "Today is a very warm day."

"Yes," said the man. "It's very warm. I'm not used to warm weather. I like cold weather."

Madge smiled. She said, "It's never cold here."

"No," said the man. He took a red **handkerchief** out of his pocket and wiped his face with it.

The man said, "I'm looking for my sister. Her name is Pat Johnson. She lives somewhere around here."

Madge said, "You must be her brother from Alaska."

"Yes," said the man. "My name is Skiff Miller. This visit is a surprise. My sister doesn't know I'm here."

"She lives nearby," said Walt. "Do you see that big tree over there? There's a little **path** near the tree. Walk up the path. Her house is the first one on the right."

"Thank you," Miller said.

The man started to leave. Madge said, "We'd like to visit you while you're here. We'd like to hear about Alaska."

Walt said, "Maybe you can have dinner with us some day."

"Thanks again," Skiff Miller said. "But I will be here for just one day. I'm leaving tomorrow. I have important business in Alaska."

Just then Wolf ran across the grass. Miller stared at the dog. He kept staring.

"I don't believe it," he said softly.

Check Your Reading

Put an **X** in the box next to the correct answer.

How many questions did you answer correctly? Circle your score. Then fill in your score on the Score Chart on page 216.

Number Correct	Score
1	10
2	20
3	30
4	40
5	50
6	60
7	70
8	80
9	90
10	100

Reading Comprehension

1. What was Walt fixing?
- ☐ **a.** a fence
- ☐ **b.** a door
- ☐ **c.** a window

2. Walt thought that Wolf ran after
- ☐ **a.** a man.
- ☐ **b.** a rabbit.
- ☐ **c.** another dog.

3. Skiff Miller was very
- ☐ **a.** short.
- ☐ **b.** tall.
- ☐ **c.** thin.

4. What color was Miller's beard?
- ☐ **a.** red
- ☐ **b.** black
- ☐ **c.** brown

5. Miller liked
- ☐ **a.** warm weather.
- ☐ **b.** hot weather.
- ☐ **c.** cold weather.

6. Miller was staying for
- ☐ **a.** one day.
- ☐ **b.** five days.
- ☐ **c.** two weeks.

Vocabulary

7. Miller took a handkerchief out of his pocket and wiped his face with it. What is a *handkerchief*?
- ☐ **a.** a piece of cloth
- ☐ **b.** a piece of wood
- ☐ **c.** a paper bag

8. Walt told Miller to walk up the path. A *path* is a
- ☐ **a.** hill.
- ☐ **b.** house.
- ☐ **c.** road.

Idioms

9. Madge and Walt took long walks with Wolf. The idiom *take a walk* means
- ☐ **a.** look for a place to walk.
- ☐ **b.** go for a walk.
- ☐ **c.** to be tired from walking.

10. Madge said that Wolf would catch up with them later. When you *catch up* with someone, you
- ☐ **a.** make fun of someone.
- ☐ **b.** play a game with someone.
- ☐ **c.** meet someone.

Understanding the Story

Exercise A ~ Checking Comprehension

Answer each question by writing a complete sentence. Begin each sentence with a capital letter, and end each sentence with a period. You may use the line numbers in parentheses to help you.

1. How often did Madge and Walt feed Wolf ? (1)

2. What did Walt have in his hand? (5)

3. What was Walt fixing? (6)

4. What was Skiff Miller holding in his hand? (26)

5. What did Miller take out of his pocket? (31)

6. What did Miller do with the handkerchief ? (32)

7. Who was Miller looking for? (33)

8. Why was Miller staying for just one day? (46)

Exercise B ~ Building Sentences

Make sentences by adding the correct letter.

1. ______ Madge and Walt took	**a.** on top of a large rock.
2. ______ Wolf was sitting	**b.** very strong.
3. ______ The man came out of	**c.** long walks with Wolf.
4. ______ Skiff Miller looked	**d.** the woods.

Now do questions 5–8 the same way.

5. ______ Madge and Walt did not know	**a.** at the dog.
6. ______ Skiff Miller was holding his hat	**b.** the man.
7. ______ Walt pointed to a path	**c.** near a tree.
8. ______ Miller kept staring	**d.** in his hand.

Now write the sentences on the lines below. Remember to begin each sentence with a capital letter and to end each sentence with a period.

1. ______________________________

2. ______________________________

3. ______________________________

4. ______________________________

5. ______________________________

6. ______________________________

7. ______________________________

8. ______________________________

Exercise C ~ Adding Vocabulary

In the box are 6 words from the story. Complete each sentence by adding the correct word.

nearby	hammer	dinner
mouth	shoulders	continued

1. The dog opened his ________________.
2. Skiff Miller's ________________ were wide.
3. Their neighbor, Mrs. Johnson, lived ________________.
4. Walt used a ________________ to fix the fence.
5. Madge and Walt ________________ to walk.
6. They asked Mr. Miller to have ________________ with them.

Exercise D ~ Using Verbs Correctly

Part A

Fill in each blank using the **present tense** of the verb *to have (have, has).*

1. Skiff Miller ________________ wide shoulders.
2. He ________________ long hair.
3. He also ________________ a beard.
4. Walt told Miller, "Maybe you can ________________ dinner with us."
5. Miller said, "I ________________ important business in Alaska."

Part B

Now fill in each blank using the **past tense** of the verb *to be (was, were)*.

Remember that the past tense of the verb *to be* does not follow the usual rules. The correct way to write this verb is shown on the chart below.

Singular		**Plural**	
[one]		[more than one]	
I	was	we	were
you	were	you	were
he/she/it	was	they	were

1. Walt said, "Wolf ______________ here a minute ago."

2. The dog ______________ not very friendly.

3. Madge and Walt ______________ very surprised.

4. The man ______________ very tall.

5. He ______________ very strong.

6. His sister ______________ their neighbor.

7. They ______________ sorry he could not stay for dinner.

Exercise E ~ Adding an Adjective

Complete the sentences below by writing the correct adjective from the box. Each sentence tells something about the story. Use each adjective once.

An **adjective** is a word that tells about a noun.

adjective **noun**
Example: They lived in a *small* house.

old	**black**	**important**
warm	**large**	**tall**

1. Miller did not wear a hat because it was a very ____________ day.
2. They could not see the dog because he ran into the ____________ grass.
3. Skiff Miller had ____________ business in Alaska.
4. The man had long hair and a thick, ____________ beard.
5. The dog sat on a ____________ rock.
6. Walt was fixing an ____________ fence.

Exercise F ~ Vocabulary Review

Part A

Write a complete sentence for each word or idiom.

1. nearby ______________________________

____

2. shoulders ______________________________

____

3. continued ______________________________

____

4. handkerchief ______________________________

____

5. path ______________________________

____

6. take (or took) a walk (idiom) ______________________________

____

7. catch (or caught) up (idiom) ______________________________

____

Part B

Write about what happened in the story. Use two or more of the vocabulary words and an idiom.

Before You Read Part 3

At the end of Part 2, Skiff Miller saw Wolf. He kept staring at the dog. "I don't believe it," he said. Why do you think he was so surprised? See if you are right.

PART 3

Skiff Miller sat down on a log. He looked at the dog. Miller shook his head. "I don't believe it," he said again.

Wolf heard Skiff Miller's words. The dog ran to the man and looked at the man's hands. He licked them with his tongue. Miller reached out and patted the dog's head.

Miller looked up at Madge and Walt. "I had to sit down," Miller said. "I was very surprised."

"We're suprised, too," said Walt. "Wolf isn't very friendly. But he was friendly to you."

"Is that what you call him—'Wolf'?" asked Skiff.

"Yes," said Madge. "I wonder why he's friendly to you." She thought for a moment. Then she said, "Maybe it's because you're from Alaska. Wolf is from Alaska, too, you know."

"Yes," said Miller. "I know."

Miller reached out again and touched one of Wolf's paws. "The dog's paw feels soft," Miller said. "He hasn't pulled a sled for a long time."

"That's true," said Walt.

No one spoke for a moment. Then Madge said, "I'm surprised that Wolf let you touch him."

Skiff Miller stood up suddenly. He said, "How long have you had this dog?"

Before anyone could answer Wolf barked.

Madge and Walt were **shocked**. They never heard Wolf bark before. The dog barked again.

"Wolf never barked before," said Madge.

Miller smiled. "I have heard him bark before," he said.

Madge stared at Miller. "What do you mean?" she said. Suddenly she felt scared. "You just met Wolf."

Miller looked closely at Madge. "You're wrong about that," he said. His voice sounded angry. "This is *my* dog."

"Yes," said Miller. "This is my dog! I thought you could see that from the way he acted. He's *my* dog. His name is not 'Wolf.' His name is 'Brown.'"

"How do you know he's your dog?" Walt asked loudly.

"He is!" was the answer.

Walt looked at Miller. "You can't **prove** that," said Walt.

Miller said, "The dog is mine. I guess I should know my own dog. This dog is mine. I can prove it! Watch!"

Skiff Miller turned to the dog. "Brown!" shouted Miller.

The dog turned around and looked at Miller.

"Turn!" shouted Miller. "Turn! Get ready!"

The dog turned **at once**. It stared ahead and waited.

"He knows my voice," Miller explained. "He listens to me. Turn again!" said Miller. The dog turned again.

Walt looked unhappy.

"He was my best dog," said Miller. "He was the best dog in my team of dogs."

"But you're not going to take him with you?" said Madge.

"Yes," said Miller. "I'm taking him back to Alaska."

"To Alaska?" said Walt. "To that cold, cold world? He'll suffer there."

"Yes," said Madge. "Why don't you leave him here? He likes it here! He gets **plenty** of food. And he won't have to pull a sled through the snow."

"He doesn't mind pulling a sled," said Miller. "He's strong, you know."

"But he's happy here," said Walt. "What can you give him in Alaska?"

"Work," said Skiff Miller. "I'll give him work. He likes work. And he'll have the cold and the snow. He likes them, too. He knows that life. He was born in Alaska. He grew up there."

Skiff Miller shook his head and said, "He may be happy here. But he'll be happier in Alaska."

"Well, I won't let you take the dog!" Walt said suddenly. "I don't want to talk about it. The dog is not going!"

Check Your Reading

Put an **X** in the box next to the correct answer.

How many questions did you answer correctly? Circle your score. Then fill in your score on the Score Chart on page 216.

Number Correct	Score
1	10
2	20
3	30
4	40
5	50
6	60
7	70
8	80
9	90
10	100

Reading Comprehension

1. The dog
   - ☐ **a.** ran away from Skiff Miller.
   - ☐ **b.** jumped up at Skiff Miller.
   - ☐ **c.** licked Skiff Miller's hands.

2. Skiff Miller said that the dog's paw felt
   - ☐ **a.** soft.
   - ☐ **b.** hard.
   - ☐ **c.** thin.

3. Madge and Walt were surprised that Wolf
   - ☐ **a.** was afraid of Miller.
   - ☐ **b.** was friendly to Miller.
   - ☐ **c.** tried to bite Miller.

4. Miller said that the dog's name was
   - ☐ **a.** Wolf.
   - ☐ **b.** Brown.
   - ☐ **c.** Spot.

5. Miller told Walt and Madge that he would
   - ☐ **a.** leave the dog with them.
   - ☐ **b.** take the dog to Alaska.
   - ☐ **c.** sell the dog to someone.

6. Miller said he would give the dog
   - ☐ **a.** good food.
   - ☐ **b.** a warm house.
   - ☐ **c.** work.

Vocabulary

7. Walt and Madge never heard Wolf bark before. They were shocked. The word *shocked* means
   - ☐ **a.** worried.
   - ☐ **b.** sad.
   - ☐ **c.** surprised.

8. Miller said, "This dog is mine. I can prove it!" When you *prove* something, you
   - ☐ **a.** show that you like it.
   - ☐ **b.** help it.
   - ☐ **c.** show that it is true.

9. Madge said that Wolf got plenty of food. The word *plenty* means
   - ☐ **a.** a little bit.
   - ☐ **b.** a lot.
   - ☐ **c.** the same kind.

Idioms

10. When Miller told the dog to turn, the dog turned at once. The idiom *at once* means
   - ☐ **a.** very soon.
   - ☐ **b.** after a long time.
   - ☐ **c.** slowly.

Understanding the Story

Exercise A ~ Checking Comprehension

Answer each question by writing a complete sentence. Begin each sentence with a capital letter, and end each sentence with a period. You may use the line numbers in parentheses to help you.

1. What did Skiff Miller sit down on? (1)

2. Why did Miller sit down? (6)

3. Where is Skiff Miller from? (13)

4. How did the dog's paw feel? (16)

5. Why were Madge and Walt surprised when Wolf barked? (24)

6. When Miller shouted "Turn," what did the dog do? (43)

7. Where was the dog born? (61)

8. Where did the dog grow up? (61)

Exercise B ~ Building Sentences

Build sentences by adding the correct letter.

1. ______ Wolf looked	**a.** from Alaska.
2. ______ Skiff Miller reached out and	**b.** at the man's hands.
3. ______ Madge said that the dog was	**c.** the dog bark before.
4. ______ Miller said he had heard	**d.** patted the dog's head.

Now do questions 5–8 the same way.

5. ______ Madge suddenly	**a.** angry.
6. ______ Skiff Miller's voice sounded	**b.** the dog was strong.
7. ______ The dog stared	**c.** felt scared.
8. ______ Miller said that	**d.** ahead and waited.

Now write the sentences on the lines below. Remember to begin each sentence with a capital letter and to end each sentence with a period.

1. ______________________________

2. ______________________________

3. ______________________________

4. ______________________________

5. ______________________________

6. ______________________________

7. ______________________________

8. ______________________________

Exercise C ~ Adding Vocabulary

In the box are 6 words from the story. Complete each sentence by adding the correct word.

tongue	paws	licked
team	log	suffer

1. Skiff Miller sat down on a __________.
2. The dog __________ the man's hands.
3. He licked the man's hands with his __________.
4. Miller touched one of the dog's __________.
5. Madge thought the dog would __________ in Alaska.
6. Brown was the best dog in Miller's __________ of dogs.

Exercise D ~ Using Verbs Correctly

Part A

Fill in each blank using the **present tense** of the regular verb in parentheses. The first one has been done for you.

1. When he is in Alaska, Brown ___works___ hard. (work)
2. He __________ a sled through the snow. (pull)
3. Brown always __________ to his owner. (listen)
4. When his owner says, "Turn," Brown __________. (turn)
5. Brown __________ all the time. (bark)
6. He __________ Alaska very much. (like)

Part B

The six sentences in **Exercise D, Part A**, will make a paragraph. Write the paragraph on the lines below.

Exercise E ~ True or False?

Write **T** if the sentence is true. Write **F** if the sentence is false. You may look back at the story.

1. ________ Madge said that Wolf was always friendly to everyone.
2. ________ Skiff Miller was from California.
3. ________ Miller had heard the dog bark before.
4. ________ The dog listened to Miller.
5. ________ Brown was Skiff Miller's best dog.
6. ________ The dog did not like the cold and the snow.
7. ________ The dog grew up in Alaska.
8. ________ Walt said that Miller could take the dog to Alaska.

Exercise F ~ Vocabulary Review

Part A

Write a complete sentence for each word or idiom.

1. log ______________________________

____

2. tongue ______________________________

____

3. paws ______________________________

____

4. shocked ______________________________

____

5. prove ______________________________

____

6. team ______________________________

____

7. licked ______________________________

____

8. at once (idiom) ______________________________

____

Part B

Tell what happened in this part of the story. Use two or more vocabulary words and an idiom.

____

____

____

____

____

____

Before You Read Part 4

Skiff Miller wants to take the dog to Alaska. But Madge and Walt do not want Miller to take Wolf away. What do you think will happen? See if you are right.

PART 4

Miller looked at Walt. "What? What's that?" said Miller. "What's that?"

"I said the dog isn't going with you," said Walt. "I don't believe that he is your dog. Maybe you saw him in Alaska. Maybe he pulled a sled for you once. But you can't prove that he's yours!"

Skiff Miller's mouth opened. But he said nothing. Then his face became red. He was very angry.

Walt said, "The dog listened to you. That's true. But any dog from Alaska would **obey** you. Wolf is probably worth a lot of money. That's why you want him. But you can't prove that he's yours."

"Is that so?" Miller said slowly. He stared down at Walt. Walt was much shorter than Miller. "Well, no one can stop me from taking the dog right now."

Miller raised his **fist** and took a step toward Walt.

Madge stepped between the two men.

"Maybe Mr. Miller is right," she said to Walt. "Wolf does seem to know him. And Wolf did answer to the name of 'Brown.' Wolf was friendly to Mr. Miller **right away**. And Wolf barked—for the first time! Why did he bark? I think I know. Wolf was happy because he found Mr. Miller."

Walt shook his head sadly. Then he said, "I guess you're right, Madge. Wolf isn't really 'Wolf.' His real name is 'Brown.' I guess that he is Mr. Miller's dog."

Madge turned to Skiff Miller. "Would you sell the dog to us?" she asked. "We'd like to buy him."

Miller shook his head. "I'm sorry," he said. His voice was kind. "I had a team of five dogs. Brown was the leader. He was the best dog I ever had."

Miller spoke softly. "I like that dog a lot," he said. "I care about him. When he was **stolen**, I felt sick. I have been looking for him for three years. When I saw him here, I thought I was dreaming. I was so happy. I can't sell this dog to you."

Madge suddenly said, "You say you care about the dog. But you don't!"

Skiff Miller looked surprised. He said, "What do you mean?"

"You say you care about the dog," Madge said. "Then let the dog choose where he wants to live. Maybe he wants to stay here in California. Maybe he likes California better than Alaska."

Skiff Miller said nothing.

"You say you care about the dog," said Madge. "Then do whatever makes him happy."

Miller thought about this. Then he said, "Brown was a good worker. He worked hard. He was never lazy. He's smart, too. He understands you when you talk to him. Look at him now. He knows that we're talking about him."

The dog was lying at Skiff Miller's feet. The dog's ears were standing straight up. The dog looked at Miller. Then he looked at Madge. He watched them when they spoke. He seemed to be listening.

"Yes, he worked hard," said Miller. "And I do like him."

Miller thought about this some more. Then he said to Madge, "The dog has earned the right to choose. I'll do whatever he wants."

CHECK YOUR READING

Put an **X** in the box next to the correct answer.

How many questions did you answer correctly? Circle your score. Then fill in your score on the Score Chart on page 216.

Number Correct	Score
1	10
2	20
3	30
4	40
5	50
6	60
7	70
8	80
9	90
10	100

Reading Comprehension

1. Skiff Miller's face got red because he was
   - ☐ **a.** tired.
   - ☐ **b.** sick.
   - ☐ **c.** angry.

2. Which sentence is correct?
   - ☐ **a.** Walt was stronger than Miller.
   - ☐ **b.** Walt was shorter than Miller.
   - ☐ **c.** Walt was taller than Miller.

3. Madge said Wolf barked because he was
   - ☐ **a.** happy.
   - ☐ **b.** sad.
   - ☐ **c.** angry.

4. Madge asked Skiff Miller if he would
   - ☐ **a.** give the dog to them.
   - ☐ **b.** let them have the dog for a week.
   - ☐ **c.** sell the dog to them.

5. Miller looked for the dog for
   - ☐ **a.** three years.
   - ☐ **b.** five years.
   - ☐ **c.** ten years.

6. Brown was
   - ☐ **a.** very lazy.
   - ☐ **b.** a good worker.
   - ☐ **c.** not smart.

Vocabulary

7. Walt said that any dog from Alaska would obey Miller. When you *obey*, you
   - ☐ **a.** do what you are told.
   - ☐ **b.** do not listen.
   - ☐ **c.** run away quickly.

8. When the dog was stolen, Miller felt sick. When something is *stolen*, it is
   - ☐ **a.** lost.
   - ☐ **b.** found.
   - ☐ **c.** taken away.

9. Miller raised his fist and took a step toward Walt. What part of the body is the *fist*?
   - ☐ **a.** the head
   - ☐ **b.** the hand
   - ☐ **c.** the neck

Idioms

10. Wolf was friendly to Skiff Miller right away. The idiom *right away* means
    - ☐ **a.** at once.
    - ☐ **b.** much later.
    - ☐ **c.** never.

Understanding the Story

Exercise A ~ Checking Comprehension

Answer each question by writing a complete sentence. Begin each sentence with a capital letter. End each sentence with a period. You may use the line numbers in parentheses to find the answers.

1. Why did Skiff Miller's face become red? (7)

2. When Miller took a step toward Walt, what did Madge do? (15)

3. Why did Wolf bark for the first time? (19)

4. What was Wolf's real name? (22)

5. How did Miller feel when Wolf was stolen? (30)

6. How long did Miller look for Wolf? (30)

7. What did the dog do while Miller and Madge were speaking? (48)

Exercise B ~ Building Sentences

Make sentences by adding the correct letter.

1. ______ Walt thought that any dog from Alaska
2. ______ Skiff Miller
3. ______ Madge asked Miller if he would
4. ______ Brown was the

a. best dog Miller ever had.
b. sell the dog to them.
c. stared down at Walt.
d. would listen to Miller.

Now do questions 5–8 the same way.

5. ______ When he saw the dog, Miller
6. ______ Brown was a
7. ______ The dog's ears were
8. ______ Miller said he would do

a. very hard worker.
b. whatever the dog wanted.
c. thought that he was dreaming.
d. standing straight up.

Now write the sentences on the lines below. Remember to begin each sentence with a capital letter and to end each sentence with a period.

1. ______________________________
2. ______________________________
3. ______________________________
4. ______________________________
5. ______________________________
6. ______________________________
7. ______________________________
8. ______________________________

Exercise C ~ Adding Vocabulary

In the box are 8 words from the story. Complete each sentence by adding the correct word.

choose	understands	lazy	earned
leader	sick	worth	care

1. When he couldn't find Brown, Miller felt ______________.
2. Madge said, "Let the dog ______________ where he wants to live."
3. Brown was the ______________ of a team of dogs.
4. The dog is so smart that he ______________ you when you talk to him.
5. Wolf was probably ______________ a lot of money.
6. She said that Miller didn't ______________ about the dog.
7. The dog worked hard—he was never ______________.
8. Miller said, "The dog has ______________ the right to choose."

Exercise D ~ Using Verbs Correctly

Fill in each blank using the **past tense** of the regular verb in parentheses. The first one has been done for you.

1. Walt said, "Maybe he ___*pulled*___ a sled for you once." (pull)
2. The dog ______________ to Skiff Miller. (listen)
3. Miller ______________ his fist and took a step toward Walt. (raise)
4. Madge ______________ between the two men. (step)
5. She ______________ to Miller and began to speak. (turn)
6. "Would you sell the dog to us?" she ______________. (ask)
7. Brown ______________ hard because he was not lazy. (work)
8. The dog ______________ at Skiff Miller and Madge. (look)

Exercise E ~ Picking a Pronoun

Fill in the blanks by adding the correct pronoun from the box. Each sentence tells something about the story. Use each pronoun once.

A **pronoun** is a word that is used in place of a **noun**.

Example: The *dog* (noun) was lost, and *it* (pronoun) was hungry.

I	**we**
you	**you**
he, she, it	**they**

1. Miller opened his mouth, but ________________ didn't say anything.
2. Madge was afraid the men would fight, so ________________ stepped between them.
3. Miller said, "When ________________ saw the dog, I thought I was dreaming."
4. Walt told Miller, "You say the dog is yours, but ________________ can't prove that."
5. Madge and Walt loved Wolf, so ________________ tried to buy the dog from Skiff Miller.
6. Madge said, "If you will sell the dog to us, ________________ would like to buy him."
7. Miller told Madge and Walt, "I can't sell this dog to ________________."
8. Keep reading this story to see if ________________ has a happy ending.

Exercise F ~ Vocabulary Review

Part A

Write a complete sentence for each word or idiom.

1. obey ______________________________

2. fist ______________________________

3. worth ______________________________

4. leader ______________________________

5. choose ______________________________

6. lazy ______________________________

7. earned ______________________________

8. right away (idiom) ______________________________

Part B

Tell what happened in this part of the story. Use two or more vocabulary words and an idiom.

Before You Read Part 5

In Part 4, everyone agreed that the dog had the right to choose where he wants to live. Suppose that Wolf chooses. Do you think he will he stay in California with Madge and Walt, or will he go back to Alaska with Skiff? See if you are right.

PART 5

"Yes," Skiff Miller said again. "The dog has earned the right to choose. I'll do whatever he wants."

Madge smiled. "I think that's fair," she said.

Skiff Miller shook his head. Then he said, "Don't move. Stay where you are. I'll say good-bye. Then I'll walk away. If the dog wants to stay here, he can stay. But if he wants to go with me, let him go. I won't call him. I won't say a word. Don't call him either. Don't say a word to him. Let's see what he does."

"**All right**," said Madge. Walt nodded yes.

"I'm leaving now," Skiff Miller said loudly. "Good-bye." He walked up to Madge and Walt. He **shook hands** with them. Then he began to walk away.

The dog was lying on his side. He watched the three people. He saw them shake hands. He heard Skiff Miller say good-bye.

Wolf lifted his head. He stood up. He watched Miller walk away. He waited for Miller to come back. But Miller kept walking.

Wolf ran down the road. He stopped in front of Miller. He tried to stand in Miller's way. Miller said nothing. He walked around the dog.

Wolf ran back to Walt. The dog **grabbed** Walt's pant leg with his teeth. He tried to **drag** Walt toward Skiff Miller. But Walt did not move.

Wolf let go of Walt's leg. He ran down the road toward Miller. Then he ran back to Walt and Madge. He ran up to Madge. She did not speak. She did not touch him.

The dog backed away. He turned around and looked at Miller. The man was still walking. He was moving further away.

Wolf ran down the road. Suddenly he stopped. He raised his head. He barked. He barked again. But Skiff Miller kept walking.

Wolf ran back to Walt and Madge. He barked at them. They did not move.

Wolf looked back at Miller. He watched the man. The man was at the curve at the end of the road. Wolf kept watching. Then Miller

was gone. Wolf could not see him.

Wolf lay down on his side. He did not move. He was waiting for Skiff Miller to come back. Wolf lay on his side and waited. He waited and waited.

"He's staying," said Madge. "He's staying!"

Suddenly Wolf got up. He did not look at the woman and the man. He was looking at the road. Wolf had **made up his mind**. He had chosen.

Wolf began to run. He ran down the road. He ran faster and faster. He did not look back. He ran straight ahead. A minute later, Wolf was gone.

Meet the Author

Jack London (1876–1916) grew up in San Francisco, California. London lived a very exciting life. It was filled with adventure. London loved to travel. Before he was seventeen years old, he had visited China and Japan. When gold was discovered in Alaska, London went there. London wrote more than 50 books and many short stories. London's most famous book is *The Call of the Wild*. Like "Wolf," it is about a dog from Alaska.

CHECK YOUR READING

Put an **X** in the box next to the correct answer.

How many questions did you answer correctly? Circle your score. Then fill in your score on the Score Chart on page 216.

Number Correct	Score
1	10
2	20
3	30
4	40
5	50
6	60
7	70
8	80
9	90
10	100

Reading Comprehension

1. Skiff Miller said that he would
- ☐ **a.** make the dog go with him.
- ☐ **b.** give the dog to Walt and Madge.
- ☐ **c.** let the dog choose.

2. Miller told Madge and Walt
- ☐ **a.** to call the dog.
- ☐ **b.** not to call the dog.
- ☐ **c.** to follow him.

3. When Wolf ran up to Madge, she
- ☐ **a.** spoke to him.
- ☐ **b.** touched him.
- ☐ **c.** did not speak to him or touch him.

4. What was Wolf waiting for?
- ☐ **a.** He was waiting for Miller to come back.
- ☐ **b.** He was waiting for Madge to feed him.
- ☐ **c.** He was waiting for Walt to bring him some water.

5. At the end of the story, Wolf
- ☐ **a.** stayed with Madge and Walt.
- ☐ **b.** ran after Skiff Miller.
- ☐ **c.** looked sad.

Vocabulary

6. The dog grabbed Walt's pant leg. When you *grab* some thing, you
- ☐ **a.** fix it.
- ☐ **b.** hold it tightly.
- ☐ **c.** let it go.

7. Wolf tried to drag Walt toward Miller. The word *drag* means
- ☐ **a.** pull.
- ☐ **b.** throw.
- ☐ **c.** hurt.

Idioms

8. When Miller told them what to do, Madge said, "All right." When you say *all right*, you mean
- ☐ **a.** yes.
- ☐ **b.** no.
- ☐ **c.** maybe.

9. Miller shook hands with Walt and Madge and walked away. People *shake hands* when they
- ☐ **a.** talk on the telephone.
- ☐ **b.** say hello or good-bye.
- ☐ **c.** watch television.

10. At the end of the story, Wolf made up his mind. When you *make up your mind*, you
- ☐ **a.** don't know what to do.
- ☐ **b.** choose or decide.
- ☐ **c.** feel sad.

UNDERSTANDING THE STORY

Exercise A ~ Checking Comprehension

Answer each question by writing a complete sentence. Begin each sentence with a capital letter, and end each sentence with a period. You may use the line numbers in parentheses to help you.

1. What did Skiff Miller do after he shook hands with Madge and Walt? (12)

2. What did the dog hear Skiff Miller say? (14)

3. When Wolf stood in front of Miller, what did Miller do? (18)

4. What happened when the dog tried to drag Walt toward Miller? (20)

5. What happened when the dog ran up to Madge? (23)

6. Who was Wolf waiting for? (34)

7. What did Wolf do at the end of the story? (41)

Exercise B ~ Building Sentences

Build sentences by adding the correct letter.

1. ______ The dog was		**a.** shake hands.
2. ______ Wolf saw the three people		**b.** the end of the road.
3. ______ Miller walked		**c.** lying on his side.
4. ______ The man was at		**d.** around the dog.

Now do questions 5–8 the same way.

5. ______ Wolf could not		**a.** the woman and the man.
6. ______ Madge thought that Wolf		**b.** faster and faster down the road.
7. ______ The dog did not look at		**c.** was staying.
8. ______ He ran		**d.** see the man.

Now write the sentences on the lines below. Remember to begin each sentence with a capital letter and to end each sentence with a period.

1. ______________________________

2. ______________________________

3. ______________________________

4. ______________________________

5. ______________________________

6. ______________________________

7. ______________________________

8. ______________________________

Exercise C ~ Adding Vocabulary

In the box are 6 words from the story. Complete each sentence by adding the correct word.

straight	minute	teeth
curve	suddenly	nodded

1. The dog ran ________________ ahead.
2. Wolf ________________ stopped running and raised his head.
3. Skiff Miller came to the ________________ at the end of the road.
4. The dog held on to Walt's pant leg with his ________________.
5. Walt ________________ yes.
6. A ________________ later, Wolf was gone.

Exercise D ~ Using Verbs Correctly

Fill in each blank using the **past tense** of the irregular verb in parentheses. The first one has been done for you.

1. The dog ____ran____ down the road. (run)
2. Wolf ________________ the man say good-bye. (hear)
3. He ________________ Skiff Miller leave. (see)
4. Suddenly the dog ________________ up. (get)
5. "I think that's fair," Madge ________________. (say)
6. Wolf lifted his head and ________________ up. (stand)

Exercise E ~ Putting Words in Order

Make sentences by putting the words in the correct order. Write each sentence on the line. The first one has been done for you.

1. lifted / head / his / Wolf

   Wolf lifted his head.

2. ran / the / road / Wolf / down

3. not / Walt / move /did

4. hands / shook / Miller / them / with

5. him / Madge / to / not / speak / did

6. him / see / could / not / Wolf

7. look / Wolf / not / back / did

Exercise F ~ Vocabulary Review

Part A

Write a complete sentence for each word or idiom.

1. grabbed ______________________________

2. drag ______________________________

3. curve ______________________________

4. nodded ______________________________

5. suddenly ______________________________

6. all right (idiom) ______________________________

7. shake (shook) hands (idiom) ______________________________

Part B

Write about what happened in this part of the story. Use two or more vocabulary words and an idiom.

Studying the Story

A. Looking Back at the Story

Discuss these questions with your partner or with the group. Your teacher may ask you to write your answer to one or more of the questions.

- Skiff Miller said that Wolf was his dog. How did Madge and Walt know that was true?
- Why did Skiff Miller want to take the dog back to Alaska?
- Were you glad that the dog went with Skiff Miller—or did you want the dog to stay with Madge and Walt? Why?
- Why do you think Wolf went with Skiff?

B. Using a Chart to Put Events in the Right Order

The **plot** tells the important things that happen in a story. The important things that happen are called *events*. Below are some events that took place in "Wolf." Use the chart to put these events in the order they happened. Write the correct letter in each box. The first one has been done for you.

a. Skiff said he wanted to take the dog back to Alaska.

b. Madge and Walt found a hungry dog.

c. Skiff saw Wolf and said that the dog was his.

d. They gave the dog food and called the dog "Wolf."

e. One day, a man named Skiff Miller came to town.

f. The dog chose to go with Skiff Miller.

g. Everyone agreed to let the dog choose whether to go or stay.

Thinking About Literature

1. Write a paragraph that tells the **plot** of "Wolf." Use the events in the chart you completed to help you. If you wish, add some events that are not on the chart.

2. Now it's time to write *your* ending to the story. At the end of Part 3, Skiff Miller said that Wolf was his dog. He said, "I'm taking him back to Alaska." But Walt told Skiff, "I won't let you take the dog. The dog is not going." Suppose that they do *not* agree to let Wolf choose. What do you think will happen? On the lines below, write your own ending to the story.

Unit 2

Crucita

By Manuela Williams Crosno

Getting Ready to Read

1. The Story and You

In this story, you will meet Crucita. As you will see, Crucita is very kind. She is always very helpful. Tell about a time when someone helped *you*. If you wish, tell about a time when you helped someone else.

2. Learning About Literature

A **character** is someone in a story. When you read, there are many ways that you can learn about a character. You can learn about a character by what the character says. You can learn about a character by what the character does. Sometimes, you can learn what a character is like by what the character thinks. Remember what the character looks like. That may also be important.

3. Looking Ahead

Manuela Williams Crosno wrote this story. Most of the characters in her stories are Spanish. They lived many years ago in what is the state of New Mexico today. Look at the picture on the left. Do you think that the people live in a city or in a village? What kinds of jobs do you think the people have? What buildings do you see? Why are these buildings important? Look at the picture of the man and the girl. What do you think the girl's name is? Read on to see if you are right.

CRUCITA

BY MANUELA WILLIAMS CROSNO

PART 1

Crucita Valdéz lived in a small village called San Eliso. The village was near a river named the Rio Grande.

Crucita had two sisters. They were named Isabella and Rosita. They were very beautiful.

Crucita, however, was not beautiful. She had large black eyes. But they were always half-closed. She also walked in a very strange way.

One day Crucita was sitting on the steps of her house. She was five years old. Crucita's grandfather, Filiberto, looked at her. He said softly to himself, "Ah, Crucita. It is too bad you do not look like your sisters."

Crucita could hear very well. She said, "What do I look like, Grandpa?"

Filiberto was surprised. He did not think Crucita could hear his words.

He told Crucita, "You are kind to me. You are kind to everyone. You help your parents. You always do good things. You are a wonderful child, Crucita."

There was a church in the middle of the village. The church was the biggest building in the village. People prayed in the church. It was the meeting place for the villagers. **Every so often** there were parties in the church. The church was very important to the people of San Eliso.

The church was very old. When it rained, the roof **leaked**. Cold winds blew through the walls. The people of San Eliso wanted a new church. But the villagers were poor. They did not have much money. They could not **afford** to build a new church.

One day Sister Mary Olivia was in the church. Crucita was with her. They were looking at a book. Sister Mary Olivia was showing Crucita some words in the book.

Crucita said, "Sister Mary, I cannot see the words. The words are very small. They are too small for me to see."

Then Sister Mary **realized** that Crucita could hardly see. She was almost blind. That is why her eyes were always half-closed. That is why she walked in a strange way.

CHECK YOUR READING

Put an **X** in the box next to the correct answer.

How many questions did you answer correctly? Circle your score. Then fill in your score on the Score Chart on page 216.

Number Correct	Score
1	10
2	20
3	30
4	40
5	50
6	60
7	70
8	80
9	90
10	100

Reading Comprehension

1. Crucita Valdéz lived in a
   - ☐ **a.** big city.
   - ☐ **b.** large town.
   - ☐ **c.** small village.

2. Crucita's sisters were very
   - ☐ **a.** old.
   - ☐ **b.** young.
   - ☐ **c.** beautiful.

3. Crucita's eyes were always
   - ☐ **a.** wide open.
   - ☐ **b.** half-closed.
   - ☐ **c.** very red.

4. Filiberto said that Crucita
   - ☐ **a.** was kind and helpful.
   - ☐ **b.** loved to play games.
   - ☐ **c.** always got into trouble.

5. The church was the
   - ☐ **a.** smallest building in the village.
   - ☐ **b.** biggest building in the village.
   - ☐ **c.** newest building in the village.

6. Crucita walked in a strange way because
   - ☐ **a.** her legs hurt.
   - ☐ **b.** she was five years old.
   - ☐ **c.** she had trouble seeing.

Vocabulary

7. The church was old. When it rained, the roof leaked. When a roof *leaks*, it
   - ☐ **a.** keeps the building warm.
   - ☐ **b.** lets the rain in.
   - ☐ **c.** keeps the rain out.

8. The people of the village were poor. They could not afford to build a new church. The word *afford* means to have enough
   - ☐ **a.** time.
   - ☐ **b.** money.
   - ☐ **c.** room.

9. Crucita said that the words were very small. Then Sister Mary realized that Crucita could hardly see. The word *realized* means
   - ☐ **a.** found out.
   - ☐ **b.** forgot.
   - ☐ **c.** asked about.

Idioms

10. Every so often there were parties in the church. The idiom *every so often* means
    - ☐ **a.** sometimes.
    - ☐ **b.** once a year.
    - ☐ **c.** every morning and night.

Understanding the Story

Exercise A ~ Checking Comprehension

Answer each question by writing a complete sentence. Begin each sentence with a capital letter, and end each sentence with a period. You may use the line numbers in parentheses to help you.

1. Where did Crucita Valdéz live? (1)

   ____

2. How many sisters did Crucita have? (3)

   ____

3. Was Crucita beautiful? (5)

   ____

4. How did Crucita walk? (6)

   ____

5. Why was Filiberto surprised? (13)

   ____

   ____

6. How big was the church? (18)

   ____

7. What did the people of San Eliso want? (24)

   ____

8. What did Sister Mary find out? (32)

   ____

   ____

Exercise B ~ Building Sentences

Make sentences by adding the correct letter.

1. _____ Crucita Valdéz had
2. _____ One day Crucita was sitting
3. _____ Filiberto did not think that Crucita
4. _____ He said that she was

a. could hear his words.
b. a wonderful child.
c. on the steps of her house.
d. large black eyes.

Now do questions 5–8 the same way.

5. _____ The church was the
6. _____ It was very important to
7. _____ Cold winds blew
8. _____ Sister Mary was showing Crucita

a. some words in a book.
b. meeting place for the villagers.
c. the people of San Eliso.
d. through the walls.

Now write the sentences on the lines below. Remember to begin each sentence with a capital letter and to end each sentence with a period.

1. ______________________________
2. ______________________________
3. ______________________________
4. ______________________________
5. ______________________________
6. ______________________________
7. ______________________________
8. ______________________________

Exercise C ~ Adding Vocabulary

In the box are 6 words from the story. Complete each sentence by adding the correct word.

child	parents	middle
blind	church	prayed

1. One day Sister Mary Olivia was in the ________________.
2. Filiberto thought that Crucita was a wonderful ________________.
3. The church was in the ________________ of the village.
4. People ________________ in the church.
5. Crucita always helped her ________________.
6. She could hardly see; she was almost ________________.

Exercise D ~ True or False?

Part A

Write **T** if the sentence is true. Write **F** if the sentence is false. You may look back at the story.

1. ________ The village was near a river named the Rio Grande.
2. ________ The village was called Santa Fe.
3. ________ Crucita could not hear very well.
4. ________ The people of the village did not want a new church.
5. ________ Crucita said she could not see the words.

Part B

On the lines below, correct the three false sentences.

1. ____
2. ____
3. ____

Exercise E ~ Adding an Adjective

Part A

Complete the sentences below by writing the correct adjective from the box. Each sentence tells something about the story. Use each adjective once.

new	small	wonderful	beautiful	strange

1. Crucita Valdéz lived in a ________________ village.
2. The church was old, but the people could not build a ________________ church.
3. Since she could not see well, Crucita walked in a ________________ way.
4. Filiberto told Crucita, "You are a ________________ child."
5. Crucita's sisters were ________________.

Part B

Here are some other adjectives from the story. On the lines below, write your own sentences using these adjectives.

kind	large	old	good	cold

1. ____
____
2. ____
____
3. ____
____
4. ____
____
5. ____

Exercise F ~ Vocabulary Review

Part A

Write a complete sentence for each word or idiom.

1. parents ______________________________

2. blind ______________________________

3. prayed ______________________________

4. leaked ______________________________

5. afford ______________________________

6. realized ______________________________

7. every so often (idiom) ______________________________

Part B

Write about what happened in the story. Use two or more of the vocabulary words and an idiom.

Before You Read Part 2

Crucita has two beautiful sisters. But people do not think that Crucita is beautiful. She walks in a strange way, and she can hardly see. Do you think that Crucita is unhappy? Do you think that she does not care about other people? See if you are right.

PART 2

Crucita could not see well. Still, she was happy. She loved to play in the forest. The animals were her friends. Birds ate from her hand. Rabbits and squirrels ran to her when she called.

One morning Crucita woke up very early. At breakfast she looked worried. She said, "Papa, last night I had a strange dream. I dreamed that Ricardo and Hermano were on a mountain. They were **trapped** on the mountain. They could not get down. They were in trouble."

Ricardo and Hermano were brothers. They were very wild. They often went into the mountains.

Señor Valdéz said, "Do not worry, Crucita. I am sure that Ricardo and Hermano are all right. I am sure they are safe. You had a bad dream. It was only a dream."

That afternoon some men rode up to the house. They got off their horses. They ran up to the house. They were **in a hurry**.

Señor Valdéz met the men. "What is wrong?" he asked.

One man said, "We are looking for Ricardo and Hermano.

They are lost. We have looked for them for two days. We have not found them **so far**."

Another man said, "We thought they were fishing in a boat. We rode along the side of the river. But we did not see them. Have you seen Ricardo and Hermano?"

Señor Valdéz said, "Perhaps I can help you." He told the men about Crucita's dream. Then he called his daughter. He asked her, "Do you remember your dream? Where were Ricardo and Hermano? Where were they trapped? Where was the place?"

Crucita thought for a moment. Then she said, "They were on a little path that was very narrow. The path was like a ledge. It was near the top of a mountain. It was behind a tall waterfall."

One man said, "I know that place. Let's go!"

The men got on their horses. They rode toward the mountain. The men got to the mountain just before dark. They looked up at the

waterfall. They called up to the brothers.

A moment later they heard shouts. "Help! Help!" yelled the boys.

The men climbed up the mountain. They brought down the two brothers. Later the boys told what happened. They were climbing near the top of the mountain. Suddenly their rope broke. They fell and landed on the narrow path. Ricardo had twisted his **ankle**. Hermano had hurt his knee. They could not walk.

But now both boys were safe.

The brothers and their family thanked Señor Valdéz. "Do not thank me," said Señor Valdéz. "Thank Crucita. She is the one who saved the boys."

Check Your Reading

Put an **X** in the box next to the correct answer.

How many questions did you answer correctly? Circle your score. Then fill in your score on the Score Chart on page 216.

Number Correct	Score
1	10
2	20
3	30
4	40
5	50
6	60
7	70
8	80
9	90
10	100

Reading Comprehension

1. Crucita loved to
   - ☐ **a.** read many books.
   - ☐ **b.** play in the forest.
   - ☐ **c.** go to the store.

2. Crucita looked worried because she
   - ☐ **a.** was feeling sick.
   - ☐ **b.** had a fight with her sisters.
   - ☐ **c.** had a strange dream.

3. The men looked for Ricardo and Hermano for
   - ☐ **a.** two days.
   - ☐ **b.** two weeks.
   - ☐ **c.** two months.

4. Crucita dreamed that Ricardo and Hermano were
   - ☐ **a.** fishing from a boat.
   - ☐ **b.** walking in a valley.
   - ☐ **c.** on a little path near the top of a mountain.

5. The boys were not able to
   - ☐ **a.** walk.
   - ☐ **a.** talk.
   - ☐ **a.** move their arms.

6. Señor Valdéz said that
   - ☐ **a.** he saved the boys.
   - ☐ **b.** Crucita saved the boys.
   - ☐ **c.** the men saved the boys.

Vocabulary

7. The boys were trapped on the mountain. When you are *trapped*, you are
   - ☐ **a.** safe.
   - ☐ **b.** with friends.
   - ☐ **c.** not able to get away.

8. Ricardo fell and twisted his ankle. The word *twisted* means
   - ☐ **a.** turned.
   - ☐ **b.** fixed.
   - ☐ **c.** watched.

Idioms

9. The men ran up to the house because they were in a hurry. When you are *in a hurry*, you
   - ☐ **a.** move slowly.
   - ☐ **b.** move quickly.
   - ☐ **c.** feel happy.

10. A man said, "We have not found the boys so far." The idiom *so far* means
    - ☐ **a.** far away.
    - ☐ **b.** on any side.
    - ☐ **c.** up to now.

Understanding the Story

Exercise A ~ Checking Comprehension

Answer each question by writing a complete sentence. Begin each sentence with a capital letter, and end each sentence with a period. You may use the line numbers in parentheses to help you.

1. What did Crucita love to do? (1)
2. Who were Crucita's friends? (2)
3. Why did Crucita look worried? (5)
4. What did Crucita dream? (5)
5. Who were the men looking for? (16)
6. Where did the men ride? (30)
7. What happened to the rope? (36)
8. Who saved the boys? (41)

Exercise B ~ Building Sentences

Make sentences by adding the correct letter.

1. _______	Crucita could not	**a.**	the boys were safe.
2. _______	Ricardo and Hermano were	**b.**	see well.
3. _______	Señor Valdéz believed that	**c.**	the side of the river.
4. _______	The men rode along	**d.**	very wild.

Now do questions 5–8 the same way.

5. _______	Señor Valdéz told the men	**a.**	just before dark.
6. _______	She said the boys were near	**b.**	on the path.
7. _______	The men got to the mountain	**c.**	about Crucita's dream.
8. _______	The boys fell and landed	**d.**	the top of a mountain.

Now write the sentences on the lines below. Remember to begin each sentence with a capital letter and to end each sentence with a period.

1. ____

2. ____

3. ____

4. ____

5. ____

6. ____

7. ____

8. ____

Exercise C ~ Adding Vocabulary

In the box are 5 words and an idiom from the story. Complete each sentence by adding the correct word or words.

climbed	squirrels	all right
remember	narrow	ledge

1. Rabbits and ________________ ran to Crucita when she called.
2. Señor Valdéz thought that Ricardo and Hermano were ________________.
3. He asked Crucita, "Do you ________________ your dream?"
4. The men ________________ up the mountain and found the boys.
5. The boys were on a little path that was like a ________________.
6. The path was not wide; it was ________________.

Exercise D ~ Using Verbs Correctly

Fill in each blank using the **past tense** of the irregular verb in parentheses.

1. Birds ________________ from Crucita's hand. (eat)
2. One morning Crucita ________________ up very early. (wake)
3. That afternoon some men ________________ up to the house. (ride)
4. Señor Valdéz ________________ the men. (meet)
5. They ________________ not see Ricardo or Hermano. (do)
6. The men ________________ the brothers down from the mountain. (bring)
7. The boys said that their rope ________________. (break)

Exercise E ~ Changing Statements to Questions

Change each statement to a question that begins with *Who*. Put a question mark at the end of each question. The first one has been done for you.

1. Crucita could not see well.

   Who could not see well?

2. Rabbits and squirrels ran to Crucita when she called.

3. Ricardo and Hermano were brothers.

4. Señor Valdéz told Crucita not to worry.

5. That afternoon some men rode up to the house.

6. The boys told them what happened.

7. The brothers and their family thanked Señor Valdéz.

Exercise F ~ Vocabulary Review

Part A

Write a complete sentence for each word or idiom.

1. squirrels ______________________________

____

2. narrow ______________________________

____

3. climbed ______________________________

____

4. ledge ______________________________

____

5. trapped ______________________________

____

6. twisted ______________________________

____

7. in a hurry (idiom) ______________________________

____

8. so far (idiom) ______________________________

____

Part B

Write about what happened in the story. Use two or more vocabulary words and an idiom.

____

____

____

____

____

____

____

Before You Read Part 3

In Part 2, Crucita had a dream about Ricardo and Hermano. Her dream saved their lives. What else might Crucita do that would help the people of the village? See if you are right.

PART 3

It was a day in spring. Crucita was eating dinner with her parents. Suddenly Crucita said, "I think we should plant the crops[1] soon. I think we should plant them next week."

Crucita's father was surprised. "Next week?" he said. "That is very early."

"Yes," said Crucita.

Crucita's mother asked, "Why should we plant so early this year?"

"I do not know," said Crucita. "But I think it is a good idea."

Señor Valdéz thought for a moment. He turned to his wife. "We never plant so early," he said. "But let us listen to Crucita."

The next week Señor Valdéz began to plant his crops. A neighbor saw him and said, "Why are you planting so early?"

Señor Valdéz told him what Crucita had said.

"You must be joking," said the neighbor. "You are planting now because of Crucita?"

"Yes," said Señor Valdéz.

"I see," said the neighbor. At first he thought Señor Valdéz was wrong to plant so early. But then he thought about Crucita. He had heard about her dream. He remembered how she saved Ricardo and Hermano.

The next day he began to plant his crops.

Before long all the farmers in the village were planting their crops.

Everything grew very well that year. Everything came up early. One by one the farmers **gathered** their crops. Finally all the crops were in.

Señor Valdéz was sitting in the living room with his wife. He was happy. He told his wife, "The crop was very good this year."

Just then Crucita's sisters ran into the house.

"Look outside!" said Isabella.

"Yes, look outside!" shouted Rosita.

Everyone ran to the window. They looked outside.

They saw a huge black cloud. The cloud was moving toward the village. **All at once** it got very dark. There was a loud crash. Then it

---

1. *crops:* plants that are grown for food

began to rain. It rained very hard. It rained harder and harder. The rain mixed with ice. The **hail** crashed down everywhere.

The hail made loud noises on the roof. It broke some windows in the house. It crashed down on the empty fields.

Then, suddenly, the terrible storm was over. The sun came out. The day began to get brighter.

Señor Valdéz said, "I am glad we planted early. The storm would have **destroyed** the crops."

Crucita was standing at the window.

"Look," she said. "A rainbow."

Everyone looked outside. They saw a beautiful rainbow in the sky.

Check Your Reading

Put an **X** in the box next to the correct answer.

How many questions did you answer correctly? Circle your score. Then fill in your score on the Score Chart on page 216.

Number Correct	Score
1	10
2	20
3	30
4	40
5	50
6	60
7	70
8	80
9	90
10	100

Reading Comprehension

1. Crucita thought they should plant the crops
   - ☐ **a.** in a month.
   - ☐ **b.** in two weeks.
   - ☐ **c.** the next week.

2. When Crucita said they should plant early, her father was
   - ☐ **a.** angry.
   - ☐ **b.** surprised.
   - ☐ **c.** happy.

3. Which sentence is true?
   - ☐ **a.** None of the other farmers planted early.
   - ☐ **b.** Some of the other farmers planted early.
   - ☐ **c.** All of the other farmers planted early.

4. Señor Valdéz told his wife that the crop was
   - ☐ **a.** very good that year.
   - ☐ **b.** very bad that year.
   - ☐ **c.** the same as last year's crop.

5. A huge black cloud
   - ☐ **a.** moved toward the village.
   - ☐ **b.** moved away from the village.
   - ☐ **c.** broke some windows in the house.

6. After the storm was over, they saw
   - ☐ **a.** the moon.
   - ☐ **b.** many bright stars.
   - ☐ **c.** a beautiful rainbow.

Vocabulary

7. After everything came up, the farmers gathered their crops. The word *gathered* means
   - ☐ **a.** threw away.
   - ☐ **b.** brought in.
   - ☐ **c.** fell over.

8. During the storm, the hail made loud noises on the roof. What is *hail*?
   - ☐ **a.** snow
   - ☐ **b.** rain
   - ☐ **c.** small pieces of ice

9. The storm would have destroyed the crops. The word *destroyed* means
   - ☐ **a.** helped.
   - ☐ **b.** warned.
   - ☐ **c.** killed.

Idioms

10. All at once, it got very dark. The idiom *all at once* means
    - ☐ **a.** suddenly.
    - ☐ **b.** later.
    - ☐ **c.** at night.

Understanding the Story

Exercise A ~ Checking Comprehension

Answer each question by writing a complete sentence. Begin each sentence with a capital letter, and end each sentence with a period. You may use the line numbers in parentheses to help you.

1. What did Crucita tell her parents at dinner? (2)

   ____

2. When did Señor Valdéz begin to plant his crops? (11)

   ____

3. What did a neighbor ask Señor Valdéz? (12)

   ____

4. When did the neighbor begin to plant his crops? (21)

   ____

5. How did everything grow that year? (23)

   ____

6. How hard did it rain? (34)

   ____

7. What did the hail break? (36)

   ____

8. After the storm was over, what did they see in the sky? (44)

   ____

Exercise B ~ Building Sentences

Build sentences by adding the correct letter.

1. ______ Crucita was eating dinner
2. ______ Her mother wanted to know why
3. ______ The neighbor had heard about
4. ______ He remembered how Crucita

a. they should plant so early that year.
b. Crucita's dream.
c. saved Ricardo and Hermano.
d. with her parents.

Now do questions 5–8 the same way.

5. ______ Señor Valdéz was sitting
6. ______ Everyone ran to the window
7. ______ The pieces of hail
8. ______ When the storm was over,

a. and looked outside.
b. the sun came out.
c. in the living room with his wife.
d. crashed down everywhere.

Now write the sentences on the lines below. Remember to begin each sentence with a capital letter and to end each sentence with a period.

1. ______________________________
2. ______________________________
3. ______________________________
4. ______________________________
5. ______________________________
6. ______________________________
7. ______________________________
8. ______________________________

Exercise C ~ Adding Vocabulary

In the box are 5 words and an idiom from the story. Complete each sentence by adding the correct word or words.

listen	joking	huge
at first	idea	crash

1. Crucita thought it was a good ________________ to plant early.
2. Señor Valdéz told his wife, "Let us ________________ to Crucita."
3. A neighbor said, "You must be ________________ to plant now because of Crucita."
4. They looked outside and saw a ________________ black cloud.
5. There was a loud ________________ and then it began to rain.
6. ________________, the neighbor thought that Señor Valdéz was wrong to plant so early.

Exercise D ~ Using Verbs Correctly

Fill in each blank using the **past tense** of the irregular verb in parentheses.

1. Señor Valdéz ________________ the neighbor what Crucita had said. (tell)
2. The neighbor ________________ that Señor Valdéz was wrong to plant so early. (think)
3. The farmers were happy because everything ________________ well that year. (grow)
4. After the storm was over, the sun ________________ out. (come)
5. The day ________________ to get brighter. (begin)

Exercise E ~ Putting Words in Order

Make sentences by putting the words in the correct order. Write each sentence on the line.

1. spring / was / It / a / day / in

 ____

2. crops / The / up / early / came

 ____

3. house / ran / sisters / Crucita's / the / into

 ____

4. rainbow / saw / beautiful / a / They

 ____

5. over / storm / terrible / was / The / suddenly

 ____

6. day / get / brighter / The / to / began

 ____

7. glad / they / early / were / planted / They

 ____

Exercise F ~ Vocabulary Review

Part A

Write a complete sentence for each word or idiom.

1. crash ______________________________

2. huge ______________________________

3. joking ______________________________

4. gathered ______________________________

5. hail ______________________________

6. destroyed ______________________________

7. at first (idiom) ______________________________

8. all at once (idiom) ______________________________

Part B

Write about what happened in the story. Use two or more of the vocabulary words and an idiom.

____

Before You Read Part 4

In Part 4, Crucita helped the people of the village again. She saved their crops. Do people still think that Crucita is not beautiful? See if you are right.

PART 4

One day Sister Mary Olivia **called on** Crucita at her house. Sister Mary asked Crucita if she would help at the church. Crucita said, "Yes. I would like to help."

Crucita kept the church clean. She always kept a candle burning. She planted a garden next to the church. She grew corn, beans, and grapes in the garden. She also planted many beautiful flowers.

Over the years many people visited the garden. It was a quiet, peaceful place. Crucita had a warm smile for everyone. She helped the old and the ill. She played with the children who came to visit her. Everyone knew and loved Crucita.

One morning Crucita went to see Sister Mary. Crucita said, "Sister, I know you sometimes go to Santa Fe. Are you going there soon?"

Sister Mary said, "Yes. I must buy some things in Santa Fe. Why do you want to know?"

Crucita said, "I would like to go to Santa Fe with you."

Sister Mary said, "Let us go today. I will speak to Father Isidro. We can leave at once."

An hour later they were ready to leave. Father Isidro came by with a wagon and a team of mules. He also brought a driver. The four people began their long **journey**.

After several hours they got to Santa Fe. The wagon stopped at the Plaza in town.

Crucita said, "I would like to walk around the Plaza."

Sister Mary Olivia said, "We will meet you here later." Then she and Father Isidro went into some stores.

Crucita had heard about the Plaza. She knew that it had many interesting shops. Crucita could not see well, so she walked very, very slowly. Still, she **bumped** into a man.

The man was sitting on a chair. He was drawing a picture of the Plaza.

"Excuse me," said Crucita.

"No, no," said the man. "It is my fault. My chair was in the way."

The man got up from his chair. Then he bowed to Crucita.

The man said, "I am an **artist**. I came here from Mexico City. I am drawing pictures of the Plaza. I also draw some of the people I see."

The man looked at Crucita. "May I draw you?" he asked.

"If you wish," said Crucita.

"Please sit here," said the man. He pointed to the chair. Crucita sat down. The man began to draw.

The man worked for a long time. Crucita sat very still. The man and Crucita spoke to each other. Crucita told him about the village of San Eliso. She told him about the old church. She told him about her garden.

Finally he was finished. An hour had passed.

Just then Crucita heard a voice. It was Sister Mary Olivia. "We are ready to go home," she said.

Crucita said good-bye to the artist. Then she joined Father Isidro and Sister Mary. They got into the wagon. Then they left for San Eliso.

Five years went by. Crucita continued to help the old and the poor. She was a friend to the young. People called her "Crucita the Good."

Then one day a letter arrived at the village. The letter came from Mexico City. A famous artist there had sent the letter. He was the man who had drawn Crucita in the Plaza. The letter said:

I know about your village. I am sending you money. Tear down the old church. Build a new church there. Do not touch the garden.

I am sending you a stained glass window.[1] *Please use it in the church.*

The new church was finished six months later. One window was made of stained glass. This window was made by the artist from Mexico City. It showed the face of a young woman. Sunlight came through the window. The face shone brightly.

People looked at the face and said, "How beautiful she is. She looks just like Crucita!"

1. *stained glass window:* a window made of colored glass

Meet the Author

Manuela Williams Crosno (1905–1997) lived most of her life in New Mexico. She loved the state. It is where all of her stories take place. Crosno usually wrote about Spanish settlers who lived on the land more than one hundred years ago. Crosno was a teacher of English for 17 years. She was also an artist and a poet. Some of her most beautiful poems can be found in the book *The Other Side of Nowhere.*

Check Your Reading

Put an **X** in the box next to the correct answer.

Reading Comprehension

1. Sister Mary Olivia asked Crucita if she would
   - ☐ **a.** go to a meeting at the church.
   - ☐ **b.** give some money to the church.
   - ☐ **c.** help at the church.

2. What did Crucita grow in the garden?
   - ☐ **a.** apples
   - ☐ **b.** oranges
   - ☐ **c.** corn, beans, and grapes

3. Crucita said she wanted to
   - ☐ **a.** walk around the Plaza.
   - ☐ **b.** meet a friend in the Plaza.
   - ☐ **c.** buy something in the Plaza.

4. The man asked if he could
   - ☐ **a.** visit Crucita.
   - ☐ **b.** draw Crucita.
   - ☐ **c.** send a letter to Crucita.

5. The artist sent money to
   - ☐ **a.** fix up the garden.
   - ☐ **b.** build a new church.
   - ☐ **c.** buy books for the church.

6. The new church was finished
   - ☐ **a.** two months later.
   - ☐ **b.** four months later.
   - ☐ **c.** six months later.

Vocabulary

7. The man said, "I am an artist. I am drawing pictures of the Plaza." An *artist* is someone who
   - ☐ **a.** buys pictures.
   - ☐ **b.** draws pictures.
   - ☐ **c.** borrows pictures.

8. Crucita could not see well, so she bumped into a man who was sitting in a chair. When she *bumped* into the man, she
   - ☐ **a.** knocked against him.
   - ☐ **b.** asked about him.
   - ☐ **c.** cared about him.

9. The four people began their journey to Sante Fe. The word *journey* means
   - ☐ **a.** trip.
   - ☐ **b.** work.
   - ☐ **c.** train.

Idioms

10. Sister Mary called on Crucita at her house. The idiom *called on* means
    - ☐ **a.** yelled at.
    - ☐ **b.** shouted to.
    - ☐ **c.** visited.

How many questions did you answer correctly? Circle your score. Then fill in your score on the Score Chart on page 216.

Number Correct	Score
1	10
2	20
3	30
4	40
5	50
6	60
7	70
8	80
9	90
10	100

Understanding the Story

Exercise A ~ Checking Comprehension

Answer each question by writing a complete sentence. Begin each sentence with a capital letter, and end each sentence with a period. You may use the line numbers in parentheses to help you.

1. What did Sister Mary ask Crucita? (2)

2. What did Crucita say to Sister Mary? (3)

3. What did Crucita plant in the garden? (5)

4. What was the artist drawing? (34)

5. What did Crucita tell the artist? (40)

6. How long did the man work? (43)

7. What did the letter ask the villagers to build? (54)

8. What was one window made of? (57)

Exercise B ~ Building Sentences

Build sentences by adding the correct letter.

1. _____ Crucita said that she was glad	**a.** visited the garden.
2. _____ She kept the	**b.** warm smile for everyone.
3. _____ Over the years many people	**c.** church clean.
4. _____ Crucita had a	**d.** to help.

Now do questions 5–8 the same way.

5. _____ Crucita played with the children	**a.** an artist from Mexico City.
6. _____ Sister Mary and Father Isidro went	**b.** was very beautiful.
7. _____ One window was made by	**c.** who came to visit her.
8. _____ The people thought that the face	**d.** into some shops.

Now write the sentences on the lines below. Remember to begin each sentence with a capital letter and to end each sentence with a period.

1. ______________________________

2. ______________________________

3. ______________________________

4. ______________________________

5. ______________________________

6. ______________________________

7. ______________________________

8. ______________________________

Exercise C ~ Adding Vocabulary

In the box are 7 words and an idiom from the story. Complete each sentence by adding the correct word or words.

wagon	at once	candle	arrived
joined	mules	famous	several

1. Crucita always kept a ________________ burning in the church.
2. Sister Mary said, "Let us go today. We can leave ________________."
3. An hour later Father Isidro came by with a ________________.
4. He also brought a team of ________________.
5. They got to Santa Fe after ________________ hours.
6. Crucita said good-bye and then she ________________ Sister Mary and Father Isidro.
7. One day a letter ________________ at the village.
8. A ________________ artist sent money to the people of San Eliso.

Exercise D ~ Picking a Pronoun

Fill in the blanks by adding the **correct pronoun** from the box. Each sentence tells something about the story.

I	we
you	you
he, she, it	they

1. The man said, " ________________ am an artist."
2. He got up from his chair. Then ________________ bowed to Crucita.
3. He told Crucita, "I would like to draw ________________."
4. Crucita told him about the church. Then ________________ told him about her garden.
5. Many people visited the garden because ________________ was a quiet, peaceful place.
6. All of them got into the wagon. Then ________________ left for San Eliso.
7. Sister Mary said, "Father Isidro will be here soon. Then ________________ can all go to Santa Fe."
8. In his letter to the people, the man said, "I am sending ________________ money for a new church."

Exercise E ~ Changing Statements to Questions

Change each statement to a question that begins with *Where*. Put a question mark at the end of each question. The first one has been done for you.

1. Sister Mary Olivia met Crucita at Crucita's house.

   Where did Sister Mary Olivia meet Crucita?

2. Crucita planted the garden next to the church.

   ____

3. Sister Mary Olivia was going to Santa Fe.

   ____

4. Crucita wanted to go to Santa Fe.

   ____

5. The wagon stopped at the Plaza.

   ____

6. Crucita wanted to walk around the Plaza.

   ____

7. The artist came from Mexico City.

   ____

8. A letter came from Mexico City.

   ____

9. They built a new church where the old church once stood.

   ____

Exercise F ~ Vocabulary Review

Part A

Write a complete sentence for each word or idiom.

1. wagon ______________________________

____

2. joined ______________________________

____

3. famous ______________________________

____

4. arrived ______________________________

____

5. several ______________________________

____

6. bumped ______________________________

____

7. artist ______________________________

____

8. called on (idiom) ______________________________

____

Part B

Write about what happened in this part of the story. Use three or more vocabulary words when you tell what happened.

Studying the Story

A. Looking Back at the Story

Discuss these questions with your partner or with the group. Your teacher may ask you to write your answer to one or more of the questions.

- Why did Crucita walk in a strange way?
- How did Crucita save Ricardo and Hermano?
- Why did the farmers in the village plant their crops early one year? Later, were they glad that they planted early? Explain.
- How did the people in Crucita's village get money for a new church?

B. Using a Chart to Tell About a Character

In each circle in the cluster map below, write one fact that describes (tells about) Crucita. One fact has already been added. You may look back at the story.

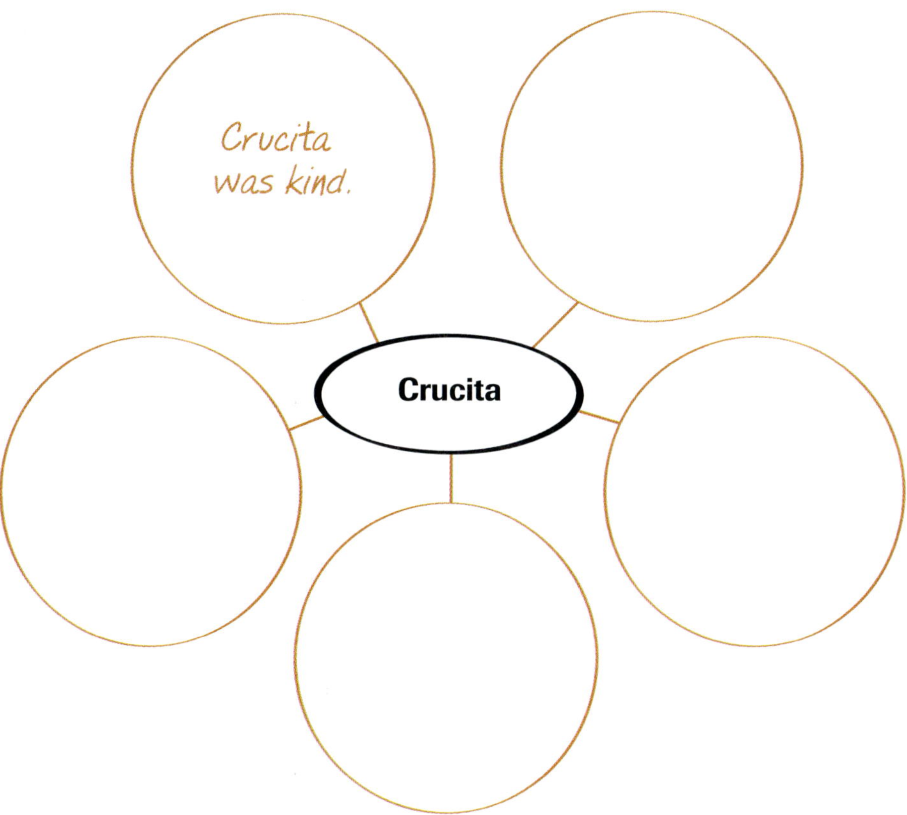

Thinking About Literature

1. Crucita is the **main character** in the story you just read. The main character is the person the story is mostly about. Look at the cluster map you completed. Use the facts in the map to help you write a paragraph that tells about, or describes, Crucita.

2. At the beginning of the story, people did not think that Crucita was beautiful. Her grandfather said, "It is too bad you do not look like your sisters." But at the end of the story, people saw the face in the stained glass window and said, "How beautiful she is. She looks just like Crucita." Probably, Crucita did so many good things that people thought she was beautiful. On each line below, list a "beautiful," or very good thing, that Crucita did. One has already been listed.

1. Crucita saved the lives of Ricardo and Hermano.

2. ______________________________

3. ______________________________

4. ______________________________

5. ______________________________

6. ______________________________

Unit 3

The Last Leaf

by O. Henry

Getting Ready to Read

1. The Story and You

In "The Last Leaf," you will meet Joanna and Sue. Joanna and Sue are friends. They are also both artists. They like to paint pictures. Tell about some of the things *you* like to do with your friends.

2. Learning About Literature

"The Last Leaf" has a **surprise ending**. This means that the story ends with a surprise. The ending is *different* from what most readers expect. O. Henry's stories always end with a surprise. See if you can guess how "The Last Leaf" will end. See if you can guess the surprise ending to the story.

3. Looking Ahead

Look at the picture on the left. See if you can find Sue and Joanna. Who else do you see in the picture? Tell what that person looks like. Do you think that he is also an artist? Do you think the story takes place in a village, a town, or a big city? Why? Read on to see if you are right.

The Last Leaf

by O. Henry

Part 1

Sue and Joanna were friends. They lived together in a small apartment. It was in Greenwich Village in New York City.

Sue and Joanna were artists. They loved to paint.

Many artists live in Greenwich Village. Most of them are poor. Sue and Joanna were poor, too. They saved their money to pay the rent. Although their apartment was small, they liked it very much. It had beautiful, big windows.

One day in November Joanna got sick. She felt very **weak**. She began to cough. She got into bed.

Day after day Joanna stayed in bed. She did not move. She did not eat. It was hard for her to breathe. Joanna stared out the window all day. **As soon as** she got up, she looked across the **alley** to the house next door. She stared at the red brick wall on the side of the house.

Joanna often said softly, "I will not get better."

One afternoon the doctor spoke to Sue. The doctor said, "Joanna is very sick. I am afraid that she may die. Joanna has pneumonia."[1]

1. *pneumonia*: an illness; a person with pneumonia often has trouble breathing

Sue was worried. She said, "What can Joanna do to get better?"

The doctor said, "There is something Joanna can do. She must *want* to live. She must *want* to get well. She must *believe* she will get well."

The doctor thought for a moment. Then he said, "What would Joanna love to do? What is important to her?"

Sue said, "Joanna is an artist. She would love to go to Italy. She would love to paint the Bay of Naples."

The doctor said, "Joanna should think about that. I will try to help her get well. I will do everything I can. But she must *want* to live."

Check Your Reading

Put an **X** in the box next to the correct answer.

How many questions did you answer correctly? Circle your score. Then fill in your score on the Score Chart on page 216.

Number Correct	Score
1	10
2	20
3	30
4	40
5	50
6	60
7	70
8	80
9	90
10	100

Reading Comprehension

1. Sue and Joanna loved to
   - ☐ **a.** write stories.
   - ☐ **b.** go to the movies.
   - ☐ **c.** paint.

2. Sue and Joanna were
   - ☐ **a.** poor.
   - ☐ **b.** rich.
   - ☐ **c.** old.

3. Their apartment was
   - ☐ **a.** large.
   - ☐ **b.** small.
   - ☐ **c.** new.

4. Day after day Joanna
   - ☐ **a.** ate a lot of food.
   - ☐ **b.** stayed in bed.
   - ☐ **c.** went to work.

5. Joanna stared at
   - ☐ **a.** her friend.
   - ☐ **b.** the walls of the apartment.
   - ☐ **c.** a red brick wall.

6. The doctor was afraid that Joanna would
   - ☐ **a.** leave the apartment.
   - ☐ **b.** get well.
   - ☐ **c.** die.

7. The doctor said it was important for Joanna to
   - ☐ **a.** want to live.
   - ☐ **b.** get out of bed.
   - ☐ **c.** watch TV.

Vocabulary

8. Joanna looked across the alley to the house next door. As used here, the word *alley* means the
   - ☐ **a.** floor of a house.
   - ☐ **b.** window.
   - ☐ **c.** narrow space between two houses.

9. Joanna got into bed because she felt weak. When you feel *weak*, you
   - ☐ **a.** feel strong.
   - ☐ **b.** do not feel strong.
   - ☐ **c.** feel very good.

Idioms

10. As soon as Joanna got up, she looked at the brick wall. The idiom *as soon as* means
    - ☐ **a.** when; just after.
    - ☐ **b.** earlier; before.
    - ☐ **c.** the next day.

Understanding the Story

Exercise A ~ Checking Comprehension

Answer each question by writing a complete sentence. Begin each sentence with a capital letter, and end each sentence with a period. You may use the line numbers in parentheses to help you.

1. What kind of apartment did Sue and Joanna live in? (1)

___

2. Where is Greenwich Village? (2)

___

3. What did Sue and Joanna love to do? (3)

___

4. What kind of windows did their apartment have? (7)

___

___

5. What did Joanna do all day? (10)

___

6. What must Joanna believe? (19)

___

7. Where did Joanna want to go? (23)

___

8. What did Joanna want to paint? (24)

___

___

Exercise B ~ Building Sentences

Make sentences by adding the correct letter.

1. ______ Many artists		a. she felt sick.
2. ______ Their apartment had		b. in bed all day.
3. ______ Joanna got into bed because		c. big, beautiful windows.
4. ______ She stayed		d. are poor.

Now do questions 5–8 the same way.

5. ______ Joanna did		a. must want to live.
6. ______ She thought she would not		b. not eat.
7. ______ Sue was		c. very worried about Joanna.
8. ______ The doctor said that Joanna		d. get better.

Now write the sentences on the lines below. Remember to begin each sentence with a capital letter and to end each sentence with a period.

1. ____

2. ____

3. ____

4. ____

5. ____

6. ____

7. ____

8. ____

Exercise C ~ Adding Vocabulary

In the box are 7 words and an idiom from the story. Complete each sentence by adding the correct word or words.

apartment	rent	brick	breathe
day after day	cough	artists	moment

1. Sue and Joanna saved their money to pay the ________________.
2. They liked the ________________ they lived in very much.
3. Many ________________ live in Greenwich Village.
4. Joanna began to ________________, so she got into bed.
5. It was hard for Joanna to ________________ because she had pneumonia.
6. Joanna stayed in bed ________________.
7. She stared at the red ________________ wall on the side of the house.
8. The doctor thought for a ________________ before he spoke.

Exercise D ~ Changing Statements to Questions

Change each statement to a question that begins with *What*. Put a question mark at the end of each question. The first one has been done for you.

1. Sue and Joanna were friends.

   What were Sue and Joanna?

2. Joanna and Sue were artists.

3. Sue and Joanna loved to paint.

4. Joanna stared out the window all day.

5. Joanna often said, "I will not get better."

6. Joanna wanted to paint the Bay of Naples.

Exercise E ~ True or False?

Part A

Write **T** if the sentence is true. Write **F** if the sentence is false. You may look back at the story.

1. ________ Sue and Joanna lived in New Jersey.
2. ________ They liked their apartment very much.
3. ________ Joanna got sick in January.
4. ________ Joanna thought she would get better.
5. ________ Joanna ate three meals every day.
6. ________ The doctor said that Joanna was very sick.
7. ________ Sue was worried about Joanna.
8. ________ Joanna wanted to paint the Bay of Naples.

Part B

On the lines below, correct the four false sentences.

1. ____
2. ____
3. ____
4. ____

Exercise F ~ Vocabulary Review

Part A

Write a complete sentence for each word or idiom.

1. alley ______________________________

____

2. weak ______________________________

____

3. cough ______________________________

____

4. brick ______________________________

____

5. artist ______________________________

____

6. breathe ______________________________

____

7. day after day (idiom) ______________________________

____

8. as soon as (idiom) ______________________________

____

Part B

Write about what happened in the story. Use three or more vocabulary words and an idiom.

Before You Read Part 2

In Part 1, the doctor said that he would try to help Joanna get well. But he told Sue that Joanna "must *want* to live." Do you think that Joanna will eat and try to get stronger? See if you are right.

PART 2

Later that day Sue went into Joanna's room. Sue took some drawing paper with her. Sue drew beautiful pictures for children's books. She used the money she earned to help pay the rent.

Sue saw Joanna lying on the bed. Joanna's eyes were wide open. She was looking out the window. Joanna was counting. Sue listened.

"*Twelve,*" said Joanna. "*Eleven. Ten. Nine.*" Joanna kept staring out the window.

Sue said to herself, "What is Joanna counting?" Sue walked across the room. She looked out the window. She looked across the alley. She saw the red brick wall on the side of the house. She saw a long **vine**. It was climbing up the brick wall.

Once there were many leaves on that vine. But now there were just a few leaves on the vine. The cold winds had blown the leaves away.

Joanna spoke again. "*Eight,*" she said. "I see only eight leaves."

"Joanna, dear," said Sue. "What are you talking about?"

Joanna turned to Sue. Joanna said, "Three days ago that vine was filled with leaves. But now there are only eight leaves on the vine. Most of the leaves are gone. I watched them fall. It will be winter soon."

Joanna turned toward the window again. "Look," she said. "There goes another leaf. See it **floating** to the ground? Now there are seven. There are seven leaves on the vine."

Sue came near the bed. "Joanna," she asked, "why are you counting the leaves?"

Joanna looked at Sue. Joanna said, "I'm waiting for the last leaf to fall. Then I will go, too."

Sue stared at her friend. "What do you mean?" Sue asked.

Joanna said, "When the last leaf falls, then I will die, too. I have known that for three days. Didn't the doctor tell you?"

"Don't be silly," said Sue. "Of course you'll get better. I spoke to

the doctor today. He told me that."

Sue said, "**Never mind** the leaves—think about yourself. Think about what you would like to do. Think about getting well! You must try to get stronger. I'll bring you some hot soup."

Joanna stared out the window. "I'm not very hungry," she said. "Look. Another leaf just fell. Now there are six."

Joanna turned to Sue. "No, I don't want any soup," she said. "I just want to look out the window. I want to see the last leaf fall. When it falls, I will die, too."

Sue said, "Joanna, please close your eyes. Don't look out the window. I'm going to draw here at the desk. Don't look at the leaves until I have finished. Please listen to me."

"Can't you draw in the other room?" Joanna asked.

Sue said, "I like the light from this window."

Sue came near the bed. She pulled the covers over Joanna. "Remember," said Sue, "don't look at those leaves."

"All right," said Joanna. "But tell me when you are finished. I want to see the last leaf fall."

Joanna closed her eyes. "I'm tired," she said. "I'm very, very tired. I want to let go of everything. I want to go sailing down, down, down, like one of those poor, tired leaves."

Check Your Reading

Put an **X** in the box next to the correct answer.

How many questions did you answer correctly? Circle your score. Then fill in your score on the Score Chart on page 216.

Number Correct	Score
1	10
2	20
3	30
4	40
5	50
6	60
7	70
8	80
9	90
10	100

Reading Comprehension

1. Which sentence is true?
- ☐ **a.** Sue sold children's books.
- ☐ **b.** Sue drew pictures for children's books.
- ☐ **c.** Sue wrote children's books.

2. When Sue came into the room, Joanna was
- ☐ **a.** reading.
- ☐ **b.** writing.
- ☐ **c.** counting.

3. There were only a few leaves on the vine because
- ☐ **a.** people picked the leaves off the vine.
- ☐ **b.** the vine was very small.
- ☐ **c.** the wind had blown the leaves away.

4. Joanna said that when the last leaf fell, she would
- ☐ **a.** feel better.
- ☐ **b.** get out of bed.
- ☐ **c.** die.

5. Sue wanted to give Joanna some
- ☐ **a.** soup.
- ☐ **b.** milk.
- ☐ **c.** water.

6. What was Sue going to do at the desk?
- ☐ **a.** read a book
- ☐ **b.** write a letter
- ☐ **c.** draw a picture

7. Joanna was waiting to see
- ☐ **a.** another doctor.
- ☐ **b.** the Bay of Naples.
- ☐ **c.** the last leaf fall.

Vocabulary

8. The vine was climbing up the brick wall. A *vine* is a kind of
- ☐ **a.** bird.
- ☐ **b.** plant.
- ☐ **c.** food.

9. A leaf was floating to the ground. As used here, the word *floating* means
- ☐ **a.** moving slowly in the air.
- ☐ **b.** burning brightly.
- ☐ **c.** breaking to pieces.

Idioms

10. Sue told Joanna, "Never mind the leaves—think about yourself." The idiom *never mind* means
- ☐ **a.** ask about.
- ☐ **b.** think about.
- ☐ **c.** don't think about.

UNDERSTANDING THE STORY

Exercise A ~ Checking Comprehension

Answer each question by writing a complete sentence. Begin each sentence with a capital letter, and end each sentence with a period. You may use the line numbers in parentheses to help you.

1. What did Sue take into Joanna's room? (1)

   ____

2. What did Sue draw? (2)

   ____

3. How did Sue use the money she earned? (3)

   ____

   ____

4. When Sue came into the room, what was Joanna doing? (5)

   ____

5. When Sue looked out the window, what did she see? (10)

   ____

6. What was Joanna waiting for? (26)

   ____

7. What did Sue want to give Joanna? (35)

   ____

8. What did Joanna want to see? (39)

   ____

Exercise B ~ Building Sentences

Make sentences by adding the correct letter.

1. _____ Sue saw Joanna
2. _____ The vine was climbing
3. _____ There were only a few leaves
4. _____ It will be

a. left on the vine.
b. winter soon.
c. lying on the bed.
d. up the brick wall.

Now do questions 5–8 the same way.

5. _____ Joanna turned toward
6. _____ Sue told Joanna to
7. _____ Joanna said that she was
8. _____ She closed her eyes

a. because she was tired.
b. not hungry.
c. the window.
d. think about getting well.

Now write the sentences on the lines below. Remember to begin each sentence with a capital letter and to end each sentence with a period.

1. ______________________________
2. ______________________________
3. ______________________________
4. ______________________________
5. ______________________________
6. ______________________________
7. ______________________________
8. ______________________________

Exercise C ~ Adding Vocabulary

In the box are 5 words and an idiom from the story. Complete each sentence by adding the correct word or words.

stronger	desk	of course
draw	leaf	rent

1. Sue said she wanted to work at the ________________.

2. She used the money to pay the ________________.

3. "Can't you ________________ in the other room?" asked Joanna.

4. Sue hoped that Joanna would get ________________.

5. Joanna watched another ________________ as it fell slowly to the ground.

6. Sue told Joanna, "You'll get better, ________________."

Exercise D ~ Using Verbs Correctly

Fill in each blank using the **past tense** of the irregular verb in parentheses.

1. Sue ________________ some drawing paper into the room. (take)

2. She ________________ pictures for children's books. (draw)

3. The cold winds ________________ most of the leaves away. (blow)

4. She said, "I ________________ to the doctor today." (speak)

5. Later that day Sue ________________ into Joanna's room. (go)

Exercise E ~ Adding an Adjective

Part A

Complete the sentences below by adding the **correct adjective** from the box. Each sentence tells something about the story. Use each adjective once.

An **adjective** is a word that tells about a noun.

adjective **noun**

Example: Sue and Joanna lived in a *small* apartment.

long	cold	red	hot	beautiful

1. Sue drew ____________ pictures for children's books.
2. The ____________ winds had blown the leaves away.
3. Sue looked at the ____________ brick wall on the side of the house.
4. A ____________ vine was climbing up the wall.
5. Sue wanted to give Joanna some ____________ soup.

Part B

Now make up your own sentences using the same adjectives.

1. ____

____

2. ____

____

3. ____

____

4. ____

____

5. ____

____

Exercise F ~ Vocabulary Review

Part A

Write a complete sentence for each word or idiom.

1. vine ______________________________

____

2. floating ______________________________

____

3. leaf ______________________________

____

4. draw ______________________________

____

5. stronger ______________________________

____

6. of course (idiom) ______________________________

____

7. never mind (idiom) ______________________________

____

Part B

Write about what happened in the story. Use three or more vocabulary words and an idiom.

____

____

____

____

____

____

____

____

____

Before You Read Part 3

Joanna said that she was counting the leaves on a vine outside her window. There were six leaves left on the vine. She said that she was going to die when the last leaf fell. In Part 3, do you think that the last leaf will fall? See if you are right.

PART 3

"Yes," said Joanna, "I'm very, very tired. I want to go sailing down, down, down, like one of those poor, tired leaves."

"Try to sleep," said Sue. "I must go downstairs now. I'm going to ask Mr. Behrman to come up here. I must draw a picture of an old man with a white beard. Mr. Behrman said that I could draw him. I'll be back right away."

Mr. Behrman was an artist who lived in the building. Behrman had been painting for more than forty years. Nobody bought his paintings. But he still dreamed of painting a great picture. He often said, "One day I will paint a great painting. I will paint a great work of art!"

People laughed at Behrman. Then he said, "I'll do it. You'll see." Meanwhile he earned money by driving a **taxi**.

Sue knocked on Behrman's door.

"Come in," he called.

The old man looked at Sue. He saw that she was very unhappy.

"What is wrong?" he asked.

Sue told him what Joanna had said.

"What?" said Behrman. "What?" he said again. "She thinks she will die because leaves fall from a vine!" Behrman rubbed his beard. "Why do you let Joanna talk that way?" he asked angrily.

Sue said, "Joanna is very ill. She is weak. She doesn't know what she is saying."

"Poor Joanna," Behrman said. "She is sick. And it is cold in New York."

Behrman thought for a moment. Then his eyes began to **shine**. "Someday I will paint a great painting," he said happily. "I will have plenty of money. Then you and Joanna can take a vacation. You can go to some place where it's warm."

Sue smiled. "Yes, Mr. Behrman," she said. "But now come upstairs with me. I want you to sit in the chair by the window. I want to draw you."

They went upstairs. Sue quietly opened the door. She looked inside. She saw that Joanna was asleep in bed. Sue and Behrman walked to the window. They looked outside. They saw the brick wall. They stared at the vine. Then they looked at each other. There was fear in their eyes.

Suddenly they heard a **tapping** at the window. They looked outside again. It was beginning to rain. Then it began to snow.

Behrman sat down in the chair. Sue began to draw him.

Sue was sleeping the next morning. Suddenly she heard Joanna's voice. Joanna was calling her.

Sue went into Joanna's room. Joanna was in bed. She was staring at the window. The shade was down. It covered the window.

"Raise the shade," said Joanna. "I want to look outside."

Sue was worried, but she slowly pulled up the shade.

It had rained all night. It had snowed **now and then**. Strong winds had blown. But there was one leaf against the brick wall. There still was one leaf! It was the last leaf on the vine.

The leaf was bright green. It had yellow edges. It hung bravely from the vine.

"It's the last leaf," said Joanna. "I'm surprised it's still there. I thought it would fall during the night. I heard the wind. It howled for hours."

Joanna turned to Sue. Joanna said, "I know the leaf will fall today. And I will die at the same time."

"Please don't say that," said Sue. "You must think about getting better."

But Joanna did not answer.

CHECK YOUR READING

Put an **X** in the box next to the correct answer.

How many questions did you answer correctly? Circle your score. Then fill in your score on the Score Chart on page 216.

Number Correct	Score
1	10
2	20
3	30
4	40
5	50
6	60
7	70
8	80
9	90
10	100

Reading Comprehension

1. Mr. Behrman sold
   - ☐ **a.** many of his paintings.
   - ☐ **b.** some of his paintings.
   - ☐ **c.** none of his paintings.

2. Mr. Behrman dreamed of
   - ☐ **a.** painting a great picture.
   - ☐ **b.** taking a trip.
   - ☐ **c.** buying a new car.

3. Sue told Mr. Behrman that she wanted to
   - ☐ **a.** borrow money from him.
   - ☐ **b.** draw him.
   - ☐ **c.** buy one of his paintings.

4. When Behrman and Sue looked out the window, they saw that
   - ☐ **a.** the vine was covered with leaves.
   - ☐ **b.** the sun was shining.
   - ☐ **c.** it was beginning to rain.

5. When Joanna looked out the window, she saw
   - ☐ **a.** one leaf.
   - ☐ **b.** two leaves.
   - ☐ **c.** many leaves.

6. The last leaf was
   - ☐ **a.** brown and dying.
   - ☐ **b.** bright green.
   - ☐ **c.** falling slowly.

Vocabulary

7. When Behrman thought about painting a great picture, his eyes began to shine. When someone's eyes *shine*, they are
   - ☐ **a.** closed.
   - ☐ **b.** red.
   - ☐ **c.** bright.

8. Suddenly they heard the rain tapping at the window. The word *tapping* means
   - ☐ **a.** a loud crash.
   - ☐ **b.** a light, quick sound.
   - ☐ **c.** someone shouting.

9. Mr. Behrman earned money by driving a taxi. A *taxi* is
   - ☐ **a.** a car.
   - ☐ **b.** a boat.
   - ☐ **c.** an airplane.

Idioms

10. It had rained all night and it had snowed now and then. The idiom *now and then* means
    - ☐ **a.** all the time.
    - ☐ **b.** sometimes.
    - ☐ **c.** never.

Understanding the Story

Exercise A ~ Checking Comprehension

Answer each question by writing a complete sentence. Begin each sentence with a capital letter, and end each sentence with a period. You may use the line numbers in parentheses to help you.

1. Where did Mr. Behrman live? (7)

   ____

2. How long had Behrman been painting? (8)

   ____

3. Who bought Behrman's paintings? (8)

   ____

4. What did Behrman dream of? (9)

   ____

5. How did Behrman earn money? (13)

   ____

6. Why did Sue want Behrman to sit in the chair by the window? (31)

   ____

7. What color was the last leaf? (49)

   ____

8. Why was Joanna surprised to see the leaf? (51)

   ____

   ____

Exercise B ~ Building Sentences

Build sentences by adding the correct letter.

1. ______	Sue was going to draw a picture of	**a.**	very unhappy.
2. ______	Mr. Behrman saw that Sue was	**b.**	Joanna was sick.
3. ______	He was sad because	**c.**	in a chair by the window.
4. ______	Sue asked Mr. Behrman to sit	**d.**	an old man with a beard.

Now do questions 5–8 the same way.

5. ______	Joanna asked Sue to	**a.**	raise the window shade.
6. ______	There still was one leaf	**b.**	fall during the night.
7. ______	Joanna thought the leaf would	**c.**	about getting better.
8. ______	Sue told Joanna to think	**d.**	against the brick wall.

Now write the sentences on the lines below. Remember to begin each sentence with a capital letter and to end each sentence with a period.

1. ______________________________

2. ______________________________

3. ______________________________

4. ______________________________

5. ______________________________

6. ______________________________

7. ______________________________

8. ______________________________

Exercise C ~ Adding Vocabulary

In the box are 6 words from the story. Complete each sentence by adding the correct word.

vacation	art	howled
shade	ill	downstairs

1. Mr. Behrman lived ________________ from Sue and Joanna.
2. He wanted them to take a ________________ in a place that was warm.
3. He hoped to paint a great work of ________________.
4. Joanna was so ________________ that she did not know what she was saying.
5. The window ________________ was down, so Joanna could not look outside.
6. Strong winds had ________________ for hours that night.

Exercise D ~ Finding Adverbs

Part A

Many adverbs (*quickly, loudly*) end in *-ly*. Circle the adverb in each sentence below.

An **adverb** usually tells about a verb. Adverbs often end with the letters *-ly.*

Example: Joanna speaks (verb) *softly* (adverb).

1. Sue quietly opened the door.
2. The leaf hung bravely from the vine.
3. She was worried, but she slowly pulled up the shade.
4. "Why do you let Joanna talk that way?" Mr. Behrman asked angrily.

Part B

Now make up a new sentence with each adverb you circled.

1. ______________________________

____

2. ______________________________

____

3. ______________________________

____

4. ______________________________

____

Exercise E ~ Putting Words in Order

Make sentences by putting the words in the correct order. Write each sentence on the lines.

1. building / Behrman / lived / the / in / Mr.

2. wall / brick / the / saw / They

3. at / was / She / window / the / staring

4. yellow / had / edges / leaf / The

5. you / want / I / sit / window / to / the / by

6. was / eyes / their / in / There / fear

7. hours / for / The / howled / wind

Exercise F ~ Vocabulary Review

Part A

Write a complete sentence for each word or idiom.

1. taxi ______________________________

____

2. shine ______________________________

____

3. tapping ______________________________

____

4. vacation ______________________________

____

5. ill ______________________________

____

6. howled ______________________________

____

7. downstairs ______________________________

____

8. now and then (idiom) ______________________________

____

Part B

Write about what happened in the story. Use three or more vocabulary words and an idiom.

Before You Read Part 4

In Part 3, it rained all night. It snowed, and strong winds blew. But one leaf still remained on the vine. Why do you think the last leaf did not fall? (Remember that O. Henry's stories end with a surprise.) See if you are right.

PART 4

All day Joanna looked out the window. All day the last leaf hung on to the vine. Evening came. Joanna stared out the window. It was darker now, but she could see the last leaf. It was still there. She saw it clearly against the brick wall.

Sue came into the room at night. She pulled down the window shade. She turned off the light.

Cold winds blew again that night. It rained. Early the next morning, Joanna said, "Raise the shade."

The leaf was still there!

Joanna kept looking at the leaf. She looked at it for a long time.

Suddenly Joanna called out, "I've been thinking, Sue," she said. "I was wrong! I was so very wrong! Something made that last leaf stay."

Joanna kept staring at the leaf. "Yes," she said. "Something made that last leaf stay. It was to show me how foolish I was. It's wrong to want to die. It's foolish and it's wrong!"

Joanna's voice got stronger. "Please bring me some soup. And I'd like some tea. And put some pillows behind my head. I want to sit up."

An hour later Joanna said, "I'd like to go to Italy someday. I'd like to paint the Bay of Naples."

The doctor came by later. He spoke to Sue in the hall of the apartment.

"Joanna is **improving**," he said. "She is getting better. But now I must hurry downstairs. I must see someone named Behrman. He's an artist, I believe. He is old and weak. He has pneumonia, too."

The doctor looked sad. He said, "Mr. Behrman is very, very sick. There is nothing we can do for him now. I must send him to the hospital.[1] He'll be more comfortable there."

1. *hospital*: a place where people who are sick go to get care

The next day the doctor spoke to Sue again. He told her, "Joanna will get well. She is out of **danger**. She is out of danger **at last**. You don't have to worry anymore."

That afternoon Sue sat down at the edge of Joanna's bed. She looked at Joanna, who was reading a book.

"I have something to tell you," Sue said. "Mr. Behrman died today. He became sick two days ago. That's when he was found in his room. His clothing and shoes were soaking wet. He was shaking from the cold.

"Mr. Behrman had been out all night. He had been outside in the rain and the snow. The police found a ladder and his brushes and his paint in the alley."

Sue stopped. She took a deep breath. Then she said, "Look out the window, dear. Look at the last leaf on the wall. Didn't you wonder why it never moved? It didn't even move when the wind blew. Oh, Joanna, it's Behrman's greatest work of art! He painted the leaf on the brick wall! He painted it there the night that the last leaf fell."

Meet the Author

O. Henry (1862–1910) is one of America's most loved short story writers. His real name was William Sidney Porter, but he used the name "O. Henry" in his writing. Although O. Henry grew up in North Carolina, he lived in New York City for many years. O. Henry loved the city. "The Last Leaf" and many of his other stories take place there. O. Henry wrote 300 stories. They all end with a surprise!

Check Your Reading

Put an **X** in the box next to the correct answer.

How many questions did you answer correctly? Circle your score. Then fill in your score on the Score Chart on page 216.

Number Correct	Score
1	10
2	20
3	30
4	40
5	50
6	60
7	70
8	80
9	90
10	100

Reading Comprehension

1. After the rain, the last leaf
- ☐ **a.** fell to the ground.
- ☐ **b.** broke into pieces.
- ☐ **c.** was still hanging from the vine.

2. Joanna asked Sue for
- ☐ **a.** some soup and some tea.
- ☐ **b.** a glass of milk.
- ☐ **c.** a piece of cake.

3. Joanna wanted to go to Italy to
- ☐ **a.** sit in the sun.
- ☐ **b.** paint the Bay of Naples.
- ☐ **c.** visit some friends.

4. The doctor said that Mr. Behrman was
- ☐ **a.** feeling very well.
- ☐ **b.** very, very sick.
- ☐ **c.** getting better.

5. Mr. Behrman had been sick for
- ☐ **a.** two days.
- ☐ **b.** a week.
- ☐ **c.** two weeks.

6. In the alley, the police found
- ☐ **a.** a letter from Mr. Behrman.
- ☐ **b.** Mr. Behrman's brushes and his paint.
- ☐ **c.** Mr. Behrman's shoes.

7. The last leaf didn't move because
- ☐ **a.** the wind couldn't reach it.
- ☐ **b.** it was very strong.
- ☐ **c.** it was painted on the wall.

Vocabulary

8. The doctor told Sue that Joanna was improving. When you *improve*, you
- ☐ **a.** get better.
- ☐ **b.** get worse.
- ☐ **c.** stay the same.

9. The doctor said that Joanna was out of danger. The word *danger* means
- ☐ **a.** money.
- ☐ **b.** harm.
- ☐ **c.** food.

Idioms

10. Joanna was getting better at last. The idiom *at last* means
- ☐ **a.** finally.
- ☐ **b.** tomorrow.
- ☐ **c.** later.

Understanding the Story

Exercise A ~ Checking Comprehension

Answer each question by writing a complete sentence. Begin each sentence with a capital letter, and end each sentence with a period. You may use the line numbers in parentheses to help you.

1. What did Joanna do all day? (1)

2. What did Joanna ask for? (16)

3. Why did Joanna want to go to Italy? (19)

4. Where was the doctor sending Mr. Behrman? (27)

5. How long was Mr. Behrman sick? (35)

6. What did the police find in the alley? (39)

7. Where did Mr. Behrman paint the leaf? (44)

8. When did Mr. Behrman paint the leaf? (45)

Exercise B ~ Building Sentences

Build sentences by adding the correct letter.

1. ______	Although it was dark, Joanna	**a.**	to sit up.
2. ______	At night Sue pulled down	**b.**	Joanna was getting better.
3. ______	Joanna said that she wanted	**c.**	could still see the leaf.
4. ______	The doctor told Sue that	**d.**	the window shade.

Now do questions 5–8 the same way.

5. ______	Mr. Behrman had been	**a.**	the last leaf fell.
6. ______	He had been outside in	**b.**	out all night.
7. ______	The last leaf	**c.**	the rain and snow.
8. ______	Mr. Behrman painted the leaf after	**d.**	never moved.

Now write the sentences on the lines below. Remember to begin each sentence with a capital letter and to end each sentence with a period.

1. ____________________

2. ____________________

3. ____________________

4. ____________________

5. ____________________

6. ____________________

7. ____________________

8. ____________________

Exercise C ~ Adding Vocabulary

In the box are 5 words and an idiom from the story. Complete each sentence by adding the correct word or words.

foolish	comfortable	soaking
turned off	pillows	ladder

1. At night Sue pulled down the window shade and ________________ the light.
2. The doctor thought that Mr. Behrman would be more ________________ at the hospital.
3. His clothing and shoes were ________________ wet from the rain.
4. Mr. Behrman used a ________________ to reach the top of the brick wall.
5. Joanna asked Sue to put some ________________ behind her head.
6. Joanna said that it was ________________ and wrong to want to die.

Exercise D ~ Using Verbs Correctly

Fill in each blank using the **past tense** of the irregular verb in parentheses.

1. The last leaf ________________ on to the vine all day. (hang)
2. Joanna said, "Something ________________ that last leaf stay there." (make)
3. The police ________________ a ladder in the alley. (find)
4. That afternoon Sue ________________ down at the edge of Joanna's bed. (sit)
5. Mr. Behrman painted the leaf on the wall after the last leaf ________________. (fall)

Exercise E ~ Picking a Preposition

Part A

Fill in the blanks by adding the correct preposition from the box. Each sentence tells something about the story. Use each preposition once.

A **preposition** joins other words or groups of words in a sentence.

Examples: Sue and Joanna looked *at* the last leaf. (**preposition**: *at*)

The rain fell *on* the vine. (**preposition**: *on*)

for	**in**	**behind**	**out**	**to**	**against**

1. All day Joanna looked ________________ the window.
2. The police found brushes and paint ________________ the alley.
3. Later that day the doctor spoke ________________ Sue.
4. Joanna saw the leaf clearly ________________ the brick wall.
5. She looked at the leaf ________________ a long time.
6. Joanna asked Sue to put some pillows ________________ her head.

Part B

Use the prepositions in parentheses to write your own sentences.

1. (up) ____
2. (from) ____
3. (of) ____
4. (above) ____

Exercise F ~ Vocabulary Review

Part A

Write a complete sentence for each word or idiom.

1. danger ____________________

2. comfortable ____________________

3. foolish ____________________

4. improving ____________________

5. pillow ____________________

6. ladder ____________________

7. turned off (idiom) ____________________

8. at last (idiom) ____________________

Part B

Write about what happened in the story. Use three or more vocabulary words and an idiom.

Studying the Story

A. Looking Back at the Story

Discuss these questions with your partner or with the group. Your teacher may ask you to write your answer to one or more of the questions.

- Why was it important for Joanna to *want* to get well?
- Did the story have a happy ending, a sad ending, or both? Why?
- What lesson did the last leaf teach Joanna?
- O. Henry's stories end with a surprise. What is the surprise in this story?

B. Using a Chart to Show How Characters are Alike and Different

When you show how characters are alike and different, you **compare and contrast** them. Use the chart below to compare and contrast Joanna and Sue. List how the two women are *alike* and how they are *different*.

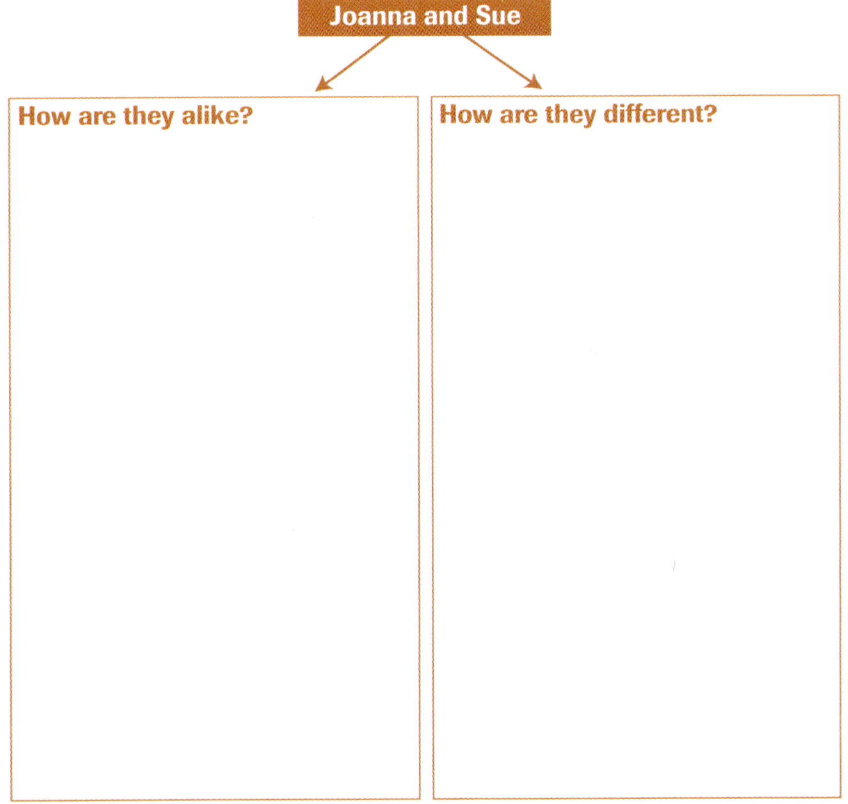

Thinking About Literature

1. What is the **surprise ending** to the story?

2. Now you can write your own surprise ending to the story. Pretend that the story ends with line 31. The doctor tells Sue that Joanna will get well. What happens then? Here are some possible new endings:

Sue explains that she painted the leaf on the wall.

Joanna painted the last leaf on the wall. Mr. Behrman helped her.

The doctor knew how important the last leaf was to Joanna. He paid an artist to paint the leaf on the wall.

Think of a surprise ending of your own or use one of the above. Then write the new ending by adding six or more sentences.

Finally, Joanna was well. One evening, she and Sue were eating dinner. They were talking.

UNIT 4

THE HERO

BY STEPHEN CRANE

GETTING READY TO READ

1. The Story and You

"The Hero" is a war story. It is about the Civil War. You have probably seen stories about war on TV or in the movies. Tell what happened in one of those stories.

2. Learning About Literature

The **setting** tells *when* and *where* the story takes place. The setting is the time and place of the story. The time of "The Hero" is during the American Civil War. That was a war between the North and the South. The war lasted from 1861 to 1865. Now you have a good idea of *when* the story takes place. See *where* the story takes place. Then you will know the *setting* of the story.

3. Looking Ahead

Look at the picture on the left. What does the picture tell you the story will be about? What are the men carrying, and what are they wearing? How do you know that the story took place a long time ago? Do you think that some exciting things will happen in the story? Read on to see if you are right.

The Hero

by Stephen Crane

Part 1

This is a war story. It is about the American Civil War.

The army had been fighting all day. The men were tired. They were hungry and thirsty. Their **uniforms** were covered with dirt.

Fred Collins turned to some men nearby. Collins was thirsty. His mouth was dry. Collins said, "I wish I had a drink. Is there any water around here?"

Nobody answered. Then someone yelled, "Look over there! There goes Turner!"

They saw a horse with a soldier on its back. The horse suddenly **rushed** forward. Then something exploded[1] near the horse. The soldier threw up his hands. He tried to cover his face. But it was too late. Smoke filled the air. There were **flames** all around.

The horse fell forward. The soldier fell to the ground. The air was filled with a terrible burning smell.

Collins shook his head and turned away. No one said a word. Everyone was quiet.

Collins looked across the field. He saw grass at the end of the field. He saw an old house that had been hit by shells. The old house was falling down. Only one wall of the house was still standing.

Collins saw a barn. He saw that the roof of the barn was burning. Near the barn was a well.

1. *exploded*: burst or blew up with a loud noise

Collins said, "I wish I had a drink." He turned to a soldier at his side. Collins said, "There's a well up there at the end of the field. I bet there's water in that well."

"Yes," said the soldier. "But how can you get it? You can't go across the field."

Collins looked at the field again. Shells exploded here and there. Pieces of earth were thrown up in the air. Grass rained down. Bullets flew.

"It's getting worse out there," the soldier said.

A shell struck the old house. There was a loud crash and the last wall fell down. When the smoke cleared, the old house was gone.

Collins said, "The well is still there. There's water in that well. I sure wish I had a drink."

The soldier said, "If you want a drink so much, why don't you go get it?" He laughed. Then another soldier laughed. Soon all the soldiers were laughing.

Collins got angry when he saw them laughing. "I will go!" he said. "I'll go in a minute if you don't **shut up**!"

The soldiers laughed again. "You say you'll go," a soldier said. "But will you run through that field? Will you run past those bullets?"

"I'm not afraid to go!" Collins said. "I tell you, I'll go!"

Then one of the men said, "I dare you to go!"

Collins stared at the man and shook his fist. "You'll see!" Collins said. Then he went to find the captain.

CHECK YOUR READING

Put an **X** in the box next to the correct answer.

How many questions did you answer correctly? Circle your score. Then fill in your score on the Score Chart on page 216.

Number Correct	Score
1	10
2	20
3	30
4	40
5	50
6	60
7	70
8	80
9	90
10	100

Reading Comprehension

1. The army had been fighting
   - ☐ **a.** for just a few minutes.
   - ☐ **b.** for only an hour.
   - ☐ **c.** all day.

2. Which sentence is true?
   - ☐ **a.** The men were not tired.
   - ☐ **b.** The men were not hungry.
   - ☐ **c.** The men were hungry and thirsty.

3. Collins said that he wanted
   - ☐ **a.** a good meal.
   - ☐ **b.** a drink.
   - ☐ **c.** to rest.

4. Near the barn was a
   - ☐ **a.** horse.
   - ☐ **b.** river.
   - ☐ **c.** well.

5. Collins got angry because the soldiers
   - ☐ **a.** laughed at him.
   - ☐ **b.** pushed him.
   - ☐ **c.** began to fight with him.

6. At the end of Part One, Collins
   - ☐ **a.** ran across the field.
   - ☐ **b.** went to find the captain.
   - ☐ **c.** got some water.

Vocabulary

7. The men's uniforms were covered with dirt. What are *uniforms*?
   - ☐ **a.** guns
   - ☐ **b.** clothing
   - ☐ **c.** food

8. The horse suddenly rushed forward. The word *rushed* means
   - ☐ **a.** moved quickly.
   - ☐ **b.** turned back.
   - ☐ **c.** stopped.

9. There were flames, and the air was filled with a burning smell. You find *flames* in a
   - ☐ **a.** barn.
   - ☐ **b.** field.
   - ☐ **c.** fire.

Idioms

10. Collins said he would go across the field if the soldiers didn't shut up. The idiom *shut up* means
    - ☐ **a.** to be quiet.
    - ☐ **b.** to close a door.
    - ☐ **c.** to leave for home.

UNDERSTANDING THE STORY

Exercise A ~ Checking Comprehension

Answer each question by writing a complete sentence. Begin each sentence with a capital letter, and end each sentence with a period. You may use the line numbers in parentheses to help you.

1. How long had the army been fighting? (1)

   ____

2. How did the men feel? (1)

   ____

3. What did Fred Collins want? (5)

   ____

4. What happened to the soldier on the horse? (13)

   ____

5. Where was the well? (21)

   ____

6. Why did Collins get angry? (38)

   ____

7. Who did Collins go to find? (46)

   ____

Exercise B ~ Building Sentences

Make sentences by adding the correct letter.

1. ______ They saw a horse with
2. ______ The soldier tried
3. ______ The old house
4. ______ Fred Collins shook his head

a. was falling down.
b. a soldier on its back.
c. and turned away.
d. to cover his face.

Now do questions 5–8 the same way.

5. ______ Collins thought there was water
6. ______ Pieces of earth
7. ______ All the soldiers
8. ______ Collins said he wasn't

a. were thrown in the air.
b. afraid to go.
c. in the well.
d. laughed at Collins.

Now write the sentences on the lines below. Remember to begin each sentence with a capital letter and to end each sentence with a period.

1. ______________________________
2. ______________________________
3. ______________________________
4. ______________________________
5. ______________________________
6. ______________________________
7. ______________________________
8. ______________________________

Exercise C ~ Adding Vocabulary

In the box are 6 words from the story. Complete each sentence by adding the correct word.

soldiers	captain	dared
worse	smoke	rushed

1. The air was filled with ________________.
2. Soon all the ________________ were laughing at Collins.
3. The horse suddenly ________________ forward.
4. "It's getting ________________ out there," a soldier said.
5. Then one of the men ________________ Collins to go.
6. Collins went to find the ________________.

Exercise D ~ Using Verbs Correctly

Fill in each blank using the **past tense** of the irregular verb in parentheses.

1. The soldier ________________ up his hands and tried to cover his face. (throw)
2. Bullets ________________ across the field. (fly)
3. Fred Collins said, "I wish I ________________ a drink." (have)
4. A shell ________________ the old house and the wall fell down. (strike)
5. Collins stared at the man and ________________ his fist. (shake)

Exercise E ~ Picking a Preposition

Part A

Fill in the blanks by adding the correct preposition from the box. Each sentence tells something about the story. Use each preposition once.

of	with	around	at	by	across

1. The men were covered ________________ dirt.
2. Collins asked, "Is there any water ________________ here?"
3. Collins shook his fist and stared ________________ the man.
4. The soldier said, "How can you get the water if you can't go ________________ the field?"
5. The roof ________________ the barn was burning.
6. The old house had been hit ________________ a shell.

Part B

Write your own sentences using the prepositions in parentheses.

1. (over) ____
2. (until) ____
3. (into) ____
4. (toward) ____

Exercise F ~ Vocabulary Review

Part A

Write a complete sentence for each word or idiom.

1. soldier ______________________________

____

2. captain ______________________________

____

3. worse ______________________________

____

4. dare ______________________________

____

5. rushed ______________________________

____

6. flames ______________________________

____

7. uniforms ______________________________

____

8. shut up (idiom) ______________________________

____

Part B

Write about what happened in the story. Use four or more vocabulary words.

____

____

____

____

____

____

____

____

Before You Read Part 2

At the end of Part 1, one of the men dared Collins to run across the field. Collins answered, "You'll see." Then he went to find the captain. Why is Collins looking for the captain? Will Collins run across the field? See if you are right.

PART 2

Collins saluted and said, "Excuse me, Captain."

"Yes?" said the captain.

"Sir," said Collins. "There is water in that well over there." Collins pointed toward the well. "I would like to get some water."

The captain was surprised. He said, "You want water from that well? You must be very thirsty."

"Yes, sir," said Collins.

The captain thought for a moment. Then he said, "Can't you wait?"

"No, sir," Collins said.

The captain looked at Collins. "Son," the captain said, "are you sure you want to do that?"

"Yes, sir," said Collins.

"Think about it," said the captain. "Think about the danger. Are you sure you want to go?"

"I want to go," said Collins.

"Well, then," the captain said, "if you want to go, you can go."

Collins saluted. "Thank you," he said.

Collins walked away. The captain shouted to him, "Collins! Bring back some water for the men . . . and hurry back!"

The captain watched Collins. He saw him talking to the men. A soldier slapped Collins on the back. Some of the men called out, "Good luck."

The captain shook his head. "I guess he's going," the captain said to himself.

Suddenly Collins felt strange. For a moment he thought he was in a dream. But the soldiers were excited. They asked **over and over**, "Are you sure you're going?"

Collins looked at them. "Of course I'm going," he said.

Collins pulled his cap down over his head. He threw back his shoulders. Then he walked quickly away.

Everybody watched. Nobody spoke.

Finally somebody said, "I don't believe it! Look at that! I didn't think he would do it!"

Another soldier asked, "What is Collins doing?"

A soldier answered, "He's going to that well over there. He's going to get some water."

The soldier was surprised. He said, "We're not dying of thirst. He's crazy!"

"Well, somebody dared him to go. Now he's doing it."

Collins stopped at the edge of the field. He looked back at the men. He was all alone. There was danger ahead, but he didn't want to turn back. He said he would do it! Now he had to cross the field! He had to face death! Then, suddenly, he didn't feel afraid.

Collins walked thirty feet into the field. He knew that the men were watching him. He looked across the field. Suddenly he saw enemy soldiers. They lifted their **rifles**. They fired. Collins heard the shots. Bullets flew by his head.

Collins ran wildly toward the well. He threw himself down on the ground and began to **crawl**. He crawled closer to the well. At last he was there! He stared into the well. It was dark in the well, but he saw water at the bottom.

Collins took the cap off the water bottle he had brought with him. There was a **cord** at the end of the bottle. Collins held on to the cord. He dropped the bottle into the well. Water flowed slowly into the bottle.

Collins lay there on the ground. Then suddenly he felt very weak. He said to himself, "What am I doing here?" He was filled with fear. He was filled with **terror**. He could not move. He thought, "I'm going to die! I'm dead! I'm dead!"

CHECK YOUR READING

Put an **X** in the box next to the correct answer.

How many questions did you answer correctly? Circle your score. Then fill in your score on the Score Chart on page 216.

Number Correct	Score
1	10
2	20
3	30
4	40
5	50
6	60
7	70
8	80
9	90
10	100

Reading Comprehension

1. Collins told the captain that he wanted to
   - ☐ **a.** go home.
   - ☐ **b.** get some water.
   - ☐ **c.** rest for a while.

2. The captain told Collins to
   - ☐ **a.** stay with the other men.
   - ☐ **b.** leave in an hour.
   - ☐ **c.** hurry back.

3. What did Collins see at the bottom of the well?
   - ☐ **a.** mud
   - ☐ **b.** water
   - ☐ **c.** nothing

4. What did Collins drop into the well?
   - ☐ **a.** a stone
   - ☐ **b.** his cap
   - ☐ **c.** an empty water bottle

5. At the end of Part Two, Collins felt
   - ☐ **a.** afraid.
   - ☐ **b.** happy.
   - ☐ **c.** brave.

Vocabulary

6. The soldiers lifted their rifles and fired. What are *rifles*?
   - ☐ **a.** guns
   - ☐ **b.** hands
   - ☐ **c.** hats

7. He got down and began to crawl. When you *crawl*, you move
   - ☐ **a.** as fast as you can.
   - ☐ **b.** up and down.
   - ☐ **c.** on your hands and knees.

8. Collins held on to the cord at the end of the bottle. A *cord* is a
   - ☐ **a.** piece of rope.
   - ☐ **b.** piece of paper.
   - ☐ **c.** piece of glass.

9. Collins could not move because he was filled with terror. The word *terror* means
   - ☐ **a.** much food.
   - ☐ **b.** much fear.
   - ☐ **c.** much joy.

Idioms

10. The soldiers asked over and over, "Are you going?" The idiom *over and over* means
    - ☐ **a.** high above.
    - ☐ **b.** very loudly.
    - ☐ **c.** again and again.

Understanding the Story

Exercise A ~ Checking Comprehension

Answer each question by writing a complete sentence. Begin each sentence with a capital letter, and end each sentence with a period. You may use the line numbers in parentheses to help you.

1. What did Collins want to get? (4)

 ____

2. What did the captain tell Collins to bring back? (18)

 ____

3. Why didn't Collins want to turn back? (42)

 ____

4. What did he see at the bottom of the well? (50)

 ____

5. What did Collins take off the water bottle? (52)

 ____

6. What did he drop into the well? (54)

 ____

7. What did Collins ask himself? (57)

 ____

8. What did he think would happen to him? (58)

 ____

Exercise B ~ Building Sentences

Make sentences by adding the correct letter.

1. ______ Collins said there was — **a.** walked quickly away.
2. ______ The captain asked Collins to — **b.** water in the well.
3. ______ For a moment Collins thought he — **c.** think about the danger.
4. ______ He pulled down his cap and — **d.** was in a dream.

Now do questions 5–8 the same way.

5. ______ Collins walked thirty feet — **a.** very weak.
6. ______ He knew that the men — **b.** himself down on the ground.
7. ______ He ran wildly toward the well and threw — **c.** were watching him.
8. ______ Then suddenly he felt — **d.** into the field.

Now write the sentences on the lines below. Remember to begin each sentence with a capital letter and to end each sentence with a period.

1. ______________________________
2. ______________________________
3. ______________________________
4. ______________________________
5. ______________________________
6. ______________________________
7. ______________________________
8. ______________________________

Exercise C ~ Adding Vocabulary

In the box are 6 words from the story. Complete each sentence by adding the correct word.

crazy	saluted	thirst
slapped	edge	enemy

1. When he saw the captain, Collins ________________.
2. A soldier ________________ Collins on the back.
3. Collins stopped at the ________________ of the field.
4. A soldier thought that Collins was ________________ to go to the well.
5. Suddenly he saw the ________________ soldiers in the distance.
6. Someone said, "We're not dying of ________________."

Exercise D ~ Using Verbs Correctly

Part A

Fill in each blank by writing the **future tense** of the verb in parentheses. Use *will* plus the verb. The first one has been done for you.

1. Fred Collins thought to himself, "I ___will go___ (go) across the field.
2. I ________________ (get) some water from the well.
3. Then I ________________ (bring) the water back to the men.
4. Everybody ________________ (drink) the water.
5. Then they ________________ (feel) much better."

Part B

On the lines below write sentences using the future tense of the verbs in the box.

speak	work	call	write

1. ____
2. ____
3. ____
4. ____

Exercise E ~ Changing Adjectives to Adverbs

Part A

Change adjectives to adverbs by adding *-ly*. Complete the sentence by writing in the correct adverb. The first one has been done for you.

1. The captain spoke to Collins in a loud voice. The captain spoke ___loudly___.
2. Collins answered in a soft voice. Collins spoke ________________.
3. Some soldiers thought that Collins was a brave man. He acted ________________.
4. Collins moved in a very quiet way. He moved ________________.
5. Will this story have a sad ending? Will it end ________________?

Part B

Add *-ly* to the adjectives in the box to make adverbs. Use each adverb in a sentence.

slow	quick	neat	nice	careful

1. ____

____

2. ____

____

3. ____

____

4. ____

____

5. ____

____

Exercise F ~ Vocabulary Review

Part A

Write a complete sentence for each word or idiom.

1. enemy ______________________________

____

2. thirst ______________________________

____

3. saluted ______________________________

____

4. rifles ______________________________

____

5. crawl ______________________________

____

6. cord ______________________________

____

7. terror ______________________________

____

8. over and over (idiom) ______________________________

____

Part B

Write about what happened in the story. Use four or more vocabulary words.

____

____

____

____

____

____

____

____

Before You Read Part 3

In Part 2, Collins reached the well. Bullets flew by his head. Collins felt weak, and he was filled with fear. Do you think that he will return safely with the water? See if you are right.

PART 3

Collins took a deep breath. Then he looked down into the well. He saw that the bottle was half full. He began to feel a little stronger.

Suddenly something exploded near him. Collins saw a flash of fire and then flames and smoke. He quickly pulled up the bottle.

Collins jumped up and looked around. He didn't know what to do. Then he saw a wooden **bucket** on the ground. It was the bucket for the well.

Collins grabbed the bucket by its chain. He **lowered** the bucket into the well. When the bucket was full, he pulled it up.

Collins held the bucket of water and began to run. He ran as fast as he could. He was filled with fear. He was afraid that a bullet would hit him. He was afraid that he would be shot dead.

Collins ran past a **wounded** man. "Young man," the soldier called. "Give me a drink of water, please."

Collins was afraid to stop. "I can't!" he screamed.

Collins kept running. His cap fell off. His hair flew wildly.

Then Collins stopped running. He turned and ran back to the wounded man.

"Here's your drink!" Collins yelled. "Here it is! Here it is!"

But the man could not lift his arm to take the water. He was falling slowly to the ground.

Collins grabbed the wounded soldier. "Here it is!" Collins said. "Here's your drink! Take it, man!"

The man did not move.

"I'll help you," Collins said. But Collins's hands were shaking. He could not keep the bucket from moving. Water splashed all over the face of the dying man.

Collins pulled the bucket away. Then he began to run again.

A few minutes later Collins was back with the men. When they saw him they cheered.

Collins offered the bucket of water to the captain.

"No," the captain said. "Let the men drink first."

Two young soldiers were the first to get the bucket. They were very happy and began to **fool around**. When one soldier tried to drink, the other soldier pulled his arm.

"Don't do that," said the first man. "You'll make me spill the water."

The other man laughed. He pulled his friend's arm again.

Suddenly there was a loud yell. The bucket crashed to the ground! Everyone was shocked! The two soldiers stared at each other. The bucket was lying on the ground—empty.

Meet the Author

Stephen Crane (1871–1900) grew up in Newark, New Jersey. Crane lived a very hard life. When he was 9 years old, his father died. His mother died when he was 18. Crane had many jobs, but he did not make much money. Often, he did not have enough food to eat. But when he was 24, Crane wrote *The Red Badge of Courage*. The book, like "The Hero," takes place during the Civil War. *The Red Badge of Courage* made Crane famous. He wrote four books of stories and some poems. But then Crane became very sick. He died at the age of 28.

Check Your Reading

Put an **X** in the box next to the correct answer.

How many questions did you answer correctly? Circle your score. Then fill in your score on the Score Chart on page 216.

Number Correct	Score
1	10
2	20
3	30
4	40
5	50
6	60
7	70
8	80
9	90
10	100

Reading Comprehension

1. When Collins looked into the well, he saw that the bottle was
   - ☐ **a.** empty.
   - ☐ **b.** half full.
   - ☐ **c.** full.

2. Collins was afraid that he would
   - ☐ **a.** fall down.
   - ☐ **b.** lose his cap.
   - ☐ **c.** be shot.

3. The wounded soldier asked for
   - ☐ **a.** some food.
   - ☐ **b.** warm clothing.
   - ☐ **c.** a drink of water.

4. Which sentence is true?
   - ☐ **a.** Collins splashed water all over the face of the dying man.
   - ☐ **b.** The dying man lifted the bucket to his mouth.
   - ☐ **c.** The dying man took a long drink.

5. The captain told Collins to
   - ☐ **a.** take the first drink.
   - ☐ **b.** be careful not to spill the water.
   - ☐ **c.** let the men drink first.

6. At the end of the story,
   - ☐ **a.** the bucket fell to the ground.
   - ☐ **b.** the captain drank from the bucket.
   - ☐ **c.** all the soldiers drank from the bucket.

Vocabulary

7. Collins saw the wooden bucket for the well. A *bucket* is
   - ☐ **a.** a large hammer.
   - ☐ **b.** a pail for carrying things.
   - ☐ **c.** a heavy box.

8. Collins lowered the bucket into the well. The word *lowered* means
   - ☐ **a.** broke.
   - ☐ **b.** pulled up.
   - ☐ **c.** let down.

9. The wounded soldier fell down. The word *wounded* means
   - ☐ **a.** hurt.
   - ☐ **b.** old.
   - ☐ **c.** tall.

Idioms

10. The two soldiers were happy and began to fool around. The idiom *fool around* means
    - ☐ **a.** to play and joke.
    - ☐ **b.** to be sorry.
    - ☐ **c.** to be angry.

UNDERSTANDING THE STORY

Exercise A ~ Checking Comprehension

Answer each question by writing a complete sentence. Begin each sentence with a capital letter, and end each sentence with a period. You may use the line numbers in parentheses to help you.

1. What did Collins see on the ground? (7)

2. When did Collins pull up the bucket? (10)

3. What was Collins afraid of? (12)

4. What did the wounded man ask for? (14)

5. Why couldn't the wounded man take the water? (21)

6. What did the men do when they saw Collins? (30)

7. Who got the bucket first? (34)

8. What happened to the bucket? (40)

Exercise B ~ Building Sentences

Build sentences by adding the correct letter.

1. ______ Collins looked down	**a.** back to the wounded man.
2. ______ When the bucket was full, he	**b.** into the well.
3. ______ Collins's cap fell off and	**c.** pulled it up.
4. ______ He turned and ran	**d.** his hair flew wildly.

Now do questions 5–8 the same way.

5. ______ The man could not lift his arm	**a.** the other soldier pulled his arm.
6. ______ A few minutes later Collins	**b.** to take the water.
7. ______ When one soldier tried to drink,	**c.** stared at each other.
8. ______ The two soldiers	**d.** was back with the men.

Now write the sentences on the lines below. Remember to begin each sentence with a capital letter and to end each sentence with a period.

1. ______________________________

2. ______________________________

3. ______________________________

4. ______________________________

5. ______________________________

6. ______________________________

7. ______________________________

8. ______________________________

Exercise C ~ Adding Vocabulary

In the box are 6 words from the story. Complete each sentence by adding the correct word.

splashed	cheered	flash
chain	offered	spill

1. Collins saw a ____________________ of fire and then flames and smoke.
2. There was a ____________________ hanging from the bucket.
3. Water ____________________ all over the face of the dying man.
4. When the men saw Collins they ____________________.
5. When he got back, Collins ____________________ the bucket of water to the captain.
6. "You'll make me ____________________ the water," the soldier said.

Exercise D ~ Changing Statements to Questions

Change each statement to a question that begins with *How*. Put a question mark at the end of each question. The first one has been done for you.

1. The bottle was half full.

   How much water was in the bottle? or

   How full was the bottle?

2. Collins began to feel a little better.

   ____

3. Collins grabbed the bucket by its chain.

   ____

4. He ran as fast as he could.

   ____

5. The two young soldiers were very happy.

   ____

Exercise E ~ Putting Words in Order

Make sentences by putting the words in the correct order. Write each sentence on the line.

1. began / feel / to / stronger / Collins

   ____

2. afraid / was / stop / He / running / to

   ____

3. its / grabbed / chain / Collins / bucket / the / by

   ____

4. man / lift / not / arm / his / The / could

   ____

5. bucket / Collins / the / away / pulled

   ____

6. the / Collins / soldier / wounded / helped

   ____

7. ground / lying / on / was / the / bucket / The

   ____

8. captain / the / to / He / bucket / offered / the

   ____

Exercise F ~ Vocabulary Review

Part A

Write a complete sentence for each word or idiom.

1. chain ______________________________

____

2. cheered ______________________________

____

3. offered ______________________________

____

4. spill ______________________________

____

5. bucket ______________________________

____

6. lowered ______________________________

____

7. wounded ______________________________

____

8. fool around (idiom) ______________________________

____

Part B

Write about what happened in the story. Use four or more vocabulary words.

____

____

____

____

____

____

____

STUDYING THE STORY

A. Looking Back at the Story

Discuss these questions with your partner or with the group. Your teacher may ask you to write your answer to one or more of the questions.

- Why did Collins go to the well? Give two reasons.
- Suppose you were the captain. Would you have let Collins go to the well? Why?
- A soldier said that Collins was crazy. Do you think that Collins was crazy, brave, or foolish? Why?
- The story ends with the bucket on the ground—empty. Why do you think the writer ended the story this way? What is he telling the reader?

B. Using a Story Map to Chart the Story

Suppose that you want to tell someone the story "The Hero." To help you, fill in the story map below.

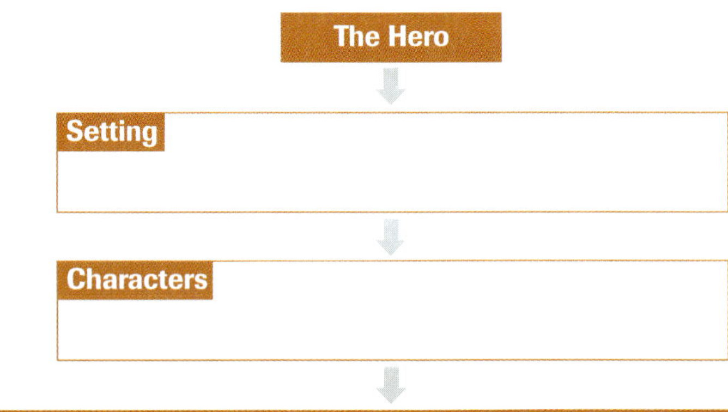

Plot (important events that take place in the story):

1.

2.

3.

4.

5.

6.

Thinking About Literature

1. Pretend that you are one of the soldiers in the battle. You want to write a letter to a friend. You want to tell your friend about Collins and the well. Use the information on the story map to help you. Write in a date between 1861 and 1865. Add your friend's name and your name.

____

(Date)

Dear ____________________

____

____

____

____

____

Your friend,

____

2. You can see why the **setting** is so important in "The Hero." Write the beginning of a story *set* on a small boat during a terrible storm. Use four or more of the words in the box in your story. They will help you tell about, or describe, the setting.

ocean	wind	deck	break	water	crash

____

____

____

____

____

____

____

RU
SIA

Unit 5
Land

by Leo Tolstoy

Getting Ready to Read

1. The Story and You

In "Land," you will meet a farmer who wanted to own a lot of land. He said, "I have always dreamed of having much land." Choose something that *you* would like to own. It should be something that you do not have now. Tell what you picked and explain why it is important to you.

2. Learning About Literature

A **motive** is the reason why a character acts the way she or he does. In "Land," Pakhom traveled to a place far away from his home. The trip was hard, and it took seven days. But Pakhom had a motive for going to that place. He wanted land, and the people there sold land for very little money. When you read the story, you will see that Pakhom did something that was not safe to do. Look for the motive, or reason, for the way he acted.

3. Looking Ahead

Look at the picture on the left. Do you think the story takes place in the city or in the country? Do the characters look happy, or do they look sad? What is the name of the country where the story takes place? The word at the bottom of the picture will help you answer this question. Notice that there is some money in a hat. What do you think the money is for? Read on to see if you are right.

LAND

BY LEO TOLSTOY

PART 1

Pakhom was a poor farmer, but he dreamed of having much land. Pakhom's farm was very small. It was less than an **acre**. Every morning Pakhom got up early and worked until it was dark. In this way he was able to save some money. Pakhom worked and saved, and he dreamed of having much land.

One day a traveler stopped at Pakhom's farm. The traveler needed food for his horse. Pakhom gave the horse some oats. Then Pakhom and the man drank tea and talked.

The man said, "I am returning from a land that is far away. It is in the south of Russia. It is called the Land of the Bashkirs."

The man told Pakhom that he had bought a piece of land from the Bashkirs. It was a very large piece of land—more than 1,500 acres. The land was **cheap**. It was very cheap. It cost only 500 rubles.

Pakhom was interested in what the traveler said.

The man said, "The Bashkirs are very stupid. They will sell you land for very little money. All you need to do is make friends with them. You must make friends with their Chief."

The man drank some more tea. He said, "It is easy to make friends with the Bashkirs. Give them some gifts. Then they will be your friends." He smiled. "I gave them some tea and some presents. This made them happy. Then they sold me a large piece of land for almost nothing."

The man told Pakhom, "Their land is very good, too. It is near a river. The earth is very rich. You can grow almost anything there."

"Do the Bashkirs own much land?" asked Pakhom.

The traveler laughed. "Oh, yes," he said. "They own many acres. They own more land than you have ever seen. If you walked all year, you could not walk from one end of their land to the other."

Pakhom shook his head and thought about the land.

"I tell you," said the traveler, "the Bashkirs are as stupid as sheep. Just give them some gifts. Then they will sell their land for very little money. They are a happy people who live in tents near the side of a river."

Pakhom was **delighted**. He thought, "I must visit the Bashkirs. I

have always dreamed of having much land. This may be my chance."

Pakhom asked, "How do you get to the Land of the Bashkirs?"

The traveler told him. Then Pakhom and the man shook hands and the traveler left.

Pakhom told his wife about the Bashkirs. Then Pakhom said, "I will go to see the Bashkirs. I will leave in the morning. You must stay here to **take care of** the farm."

The next day Pakhom and his helper started on their journey. The helper was a strong man. He pulled a heavy wooden **cart**. First they stopped at a town along the way. Pakhom bought some presents and two boxes of tea. The men put everything into the cart.

They traveled for a week. On the seventh day, they saw some tents near the side of a river. It was just as the traveler had said. The Bashkirs lived in the tents. They looked like happy people.

When the Bashkirs saw Pakhom, they came out of their tents. They stood around the visitor. The Bashkirs seemed very happy to see Pakhom. They led him into one of the best tents. They offered him a seat. They sat down around him. They gave him some tea and some food to eat.

Then Pakhom took the presents out of the cart. He gave them to the Bashkirs. He also gave everyone some tea. The Bashkirs were very happy.

Then one of the Bashkirs stepped forward. He told Pakhom, "We like you very much. You gave us presents. We would like to give you something. What can we give you? What do you want?"

"What I like," said Pakhom, "is your land. Our land is not very good. But you have plenty of land, and it is good land. I never saw land as good as this. I would like to buy a piece of your land."

The Bashkirs talked to each other. They joked and laughed. Then they were silent. The man stepped forward again.

He said, "We will gladly sell you some land. But we must wait until the Chief returns. We must ask the Chief before we can sell you the land."

Check Your Reading

Put an **X** in the box next to the correct answer.

How many questions did you answer correctly? Circle your score. Then fill in your score on the Score Chart on page 216.

Number Correct	Score
1	10
2	20
3	30
4	40
5	50
6	60
7	70
8	80
9	90
10	100

Reading Comprehension

1. The traveler stopped at Pakhom's farm to

☐ **a.** rest for the night.
☐ **b.** get food for his horse.
☐ **c.** buy another horse.

2. The traveler said that the Bashkirs lived in

☐ **a.** small houses.
☐ **b.** large buildings.
☐ **c.** tents.

3. Pakhom and his helper traveled for

☐ **a.** a week.
☐ **b.** ten days.
☐ **c.** a month.

4. What did Pakhom give the Bashkirs?

☐ **a.** tea and presents
☐ **b.** money and clothes
☐ **c.** food and horses

5. Pakhom told the Bashkirs that he wanted to

☐ **a.** stay with them for a week.
☐ **b.** buy a piece of land.
☐ **c.** teach them about farming.

Vocabulary

6. Pakhom's small farm was less than an acre. The word *acre* means the number of

☐ **a.** cows on a farm.
☐ **b.** people in a village.
☐ **c.** feet in a piece of land.

7. He paid very little. The land was cheap. Something that is *cheap*

☐ **a.** costs little.
☐ **b.** costs much.
☐ **c.** is not very good.

8. Pakhom was delighted to buy much land for very little money. The word *delighted* means

☐ **a.** very sad.
☐ **b.** very happy.
☐ **c.** very surprised.

9. The men put everything into a wooden cart. What is a *cart*?

☐ **a.** a kind of house
☐ **b.** a kind of boat
☐ **c.** a kind of wagon

Idioms

10. Pakhom's wife stayed at home to take care of the farm. The idiom *take care of* means to

☐ **a.** leave.
☐ **b.** watch.
☐ **c.** buy.

UNDERSTANDING THE STORY

Exercise A ~ Checking Comprehension

Answer each question by writing a complete sentence. Begin each sentence with a capital letter, and end each sentence with a period. You may use the line numbers in parentheses to help you.

1. Who was Pakhom? (1)

2. What did Pakhom dream of having? (1)

3. Why did a traveler stop at Pakhom's farm? (7)

4. What did Pakhom and the traveler drink? (8)

5. Where is the Land of the Bashkirs? (10)

6. How much land did the Bashkirs own? (27)

7. What did Pakhom buy in town? (43)

8. What did Pakhom give the Bashkirs? (53)

9. What did Pakhom want to buy? (60)

10. Who were the Bashkirs waiting for? (63)

Exercise B ~ Building Sentences

Make sentences by adding the correct letter.

1. _______	One day a traveler stopped	**a.** a large piece of land.
2. _______	The traveler was coming back	**b.** at Pakhom's farm.
3. _______	The traveler bought	**c.** almost nothing.
4. _______	He said that the land cost	**d.** from the Land of the Bashkirs.
5. _______	Pakhom told his wife	**e.** about the Bashkirs.

Now do questions 6–10 the same way.

6. _______	Pakhom and his helper went	**a.** their Chief.
7. _______	The helper pulled	**b.** happy people.
8. _______	The Bashkirs seemed to be	**c.** to find the Bashkirs.
9. _______	The Bashkirs gave Pakhom	**d.** a heavy wooden cart.
10. _______	The Bashkirs were waiting for	**e.** some food to eat.

Now write the sentences on the lines below. Remember to begin each sentence with a capital letter and to end each sentence with a period.

1. ____

2. ____

3. ____

4. ____

5. ____

6. ____

7. ____

8. ____

9. ____

10. ____

Exercise C ~ Adding Vocabulary

In the box are 6 words from the story. Complete each sentence by adding the correct word.

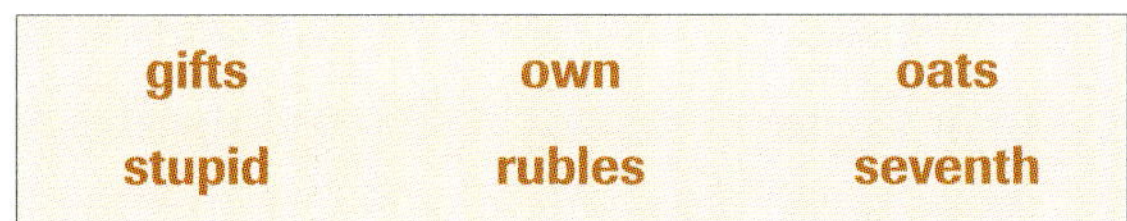

gifts	own	oats
stupid	rubles	seventh

1. Pakhom gave the horse some ________________.
2. The traveler thought that the Bashkirs were ________________ because they sold land for very little money.
3. The traveler bought the land for 500 ________________.
4. Pakhom bought some ________________ to give to the Bashkirs.
5. On the ________________ day, they saw some tents near the river.
6. Pakhom asked, "Do the Bashkirs ________________ much land?"

Exercise D ~ Using Verbs Correctly

Fill in each blank by adding the **past tense** of the regular (1–4) or irregular (5–8) verb in parentheses.

1. Pakhom ________________ of having much land. (dream)
2. One day a traveler ________________ at Pakhom's farm. (stop)
3. The Bashkirs were a happy people who ________________ in tents. (live)
4. The Bashkirs ________________ to each other about Pakhom. (talk)
5. Pakhom and the traveler ________________ some tea. (drink)
6. The traveler ________________ a large piece of land from the Bashkirs. (buy)
7. The Bashkirs ________________ their land for very little money. (sell)
8. The Bashkirs ________________ Pakhom into one of their best tents. (lead)

Exercise E ~ Picking a Pronoun

Fill in the blanks by adding the correct **object pronoun** from the box. Each sentence tells something about the story. Use each pronoun once.

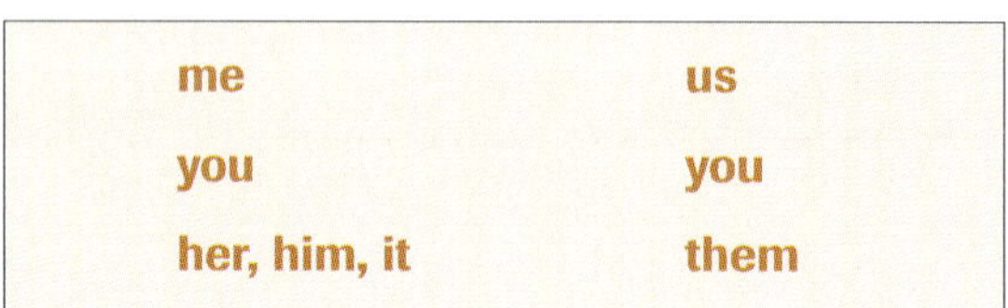

me	us
you	you
her, him, it	them

1. The traveler saw the Bashkirs and gave ________________ some tea.
2. The traveler said, "Their land is so good, you can grow anything on ________________."
3. They will sell you land if ________________ make friends with their Chief.
4. He said, "They sold ________________ a large piece of land for almost nothing."
5. When the Bashkirs saw Pakhom, they stood around ________________.
6. Pakhom told the Bashkirs, "Let me give ________________ some gifts."
7. The Bashkirs said, "We like you very much because you gave ________________ presents."
8. Pakhom spoke to his wife and told ________________ about the Bashkirs.

Exercise F ~ Vocabulary Review

Part A

Write a complete sentence for each word or idiom.

1. gifts ______________________________
____
2. own ______________________________
____
3. stupid ______________________________
____
4. seventh ______________________________
____
5. cheap ______________________________
____
6. delighted ______________________________
____
7. cart ______________________________
____
8. take care of (idiom) ______________________________
____

Part B

Write about what happened in the story. Use four or more vocabulary words.

____
____
____
____
____
____
____
____

Before You Read Part 2

At the end of Part 1, the Bashkirs said that they would gladly sell Pakhom some land. But first they had to ask the Chief. Do you think that the Chief will agree to sell Pakhom some land? If he does, do you think he will sell the land cheaply? See if you are right.

PART 2

Just then a tall man arrived. He was wearing a large fur hat and a large fur coat.

"This is our Chief," said one of the Bashkirs.

Pakhom went to the cart at once. He took out a beautiful coat and five pounds of tea. He gave these to the Chief. The Chief took them and sat down. Some of the Bashkirs came near him and **whispered** in his ear.

The Chief listened. Then he said, "I agree."

The Chief turned to Pakhom and said, "Choose whatever piece of land you like. We will sell it to you. We have plenty of land."

"What is the **price**?" asked Pakhom.

"Our price is always the same," said the Chief. "The price is 500 rubles a day."

Pakhom did not understand. He said, "How can the price be 500 rubles a day?"

The Chief laughed. "It is easy," he said. "We sell the land by the day. You can have all the land that you can walk around in a day. The price is 500 rubles."

Pakhom was surprised. He could walk around a large piece of land in a day. And 500 rubles was not too much money. He had 500 rubles in his pocket.

Pakhom said, "But in a day I can walk around a very large piece of land."

The Chief laughed. He said, "Then it will be yours!"

The Chief stopped laughing. "But there is one thing," he said. "You must return to the place you started. You must return there before the day is over. If you take longer than a day, you lose your money."

"But how will you know where I have walked?" asked Pakhom.

"That is easy," said the Chief. "Here is a shovel. Take it with you. Start at any place you like. As you walk along, dig some holes. They will tell us where you walked."

Pakhom was very happy. He said that he would leave the next morning.

That night Pakhom could not sleep. He kept thinking about the land. He thought, "I will walk around a very large piece of land. I can walk thirty or thirty-five miles in a day. I will have a huge piece of land! I'll sell some of the land, and I'll rent some of it to farmers. But I'll keep the best land for myself! That's where I'll have my farm."

Pakhom thought about the land all night. He finally fell asleep just before dawn. As soon as he closed his eyes, Pakhom had a dream. He dreamed that he was lying in his tent and that he heard someone laughing outside. He dreamed that he went outside and saw the Bashkir Chief. The Chief was laughing loudly.

In his dream Pakhom asked the Chief, "Why are you laughing?" But the Chief did not answer. Pakhom looked closely at the Chief. Then Pakhom saw that it was not the Chief who was laughing. It was the traveler who had told him about the land. The traveler was laughing loudly. The laughter grew louder and louder and louder. Pakhom suddenly woke up.

"That was a strange dream," Pakhom thought to himself.

He looked around and saw that it was early in the morning. "It's time to wake up my helper," he thought. "We must leave now."

He got up and went outside. He woke up the helper, who was sleeping in the cart. Then he went to call the Bashkirs.

"It's time to go for the land," Pakhom said.

The Bashkirs were ready, and they started to walk. Pakhom carried the shovel in his hand.

They walked until they came to the top of a hill. Then the Chief came up to Pakhom. The Chief pointed to the plain below. "Look down there," said the Chief. "Everything you can see is ours. You may have whatever land you want."

Pakhom was very happy. He could see that it was wonderful land.

The Chief took off his fur hat. He put it on the ground. "This will be the starting point," he said. "Right here." He touched the hat with his foot.

"This is where you will start," said the Chief. "And this is where you must finish. Walk wherever you like. All the land that you walk around in a day will be yours. But **keep in mind**, you must return to this spot before the sun sets!"

Pakhom took out his 500 rubles. He put them on the hat.

Then the helper walked toward Pakhom. He gave Pakhom some bread and some water. Pakhom put the bread into the pocket of his pants. He pushed the bottle of water inside his belt. He was ready to start.

CHECK YOUR READING

Put an **X** in the box next to the correct answer.

Reading Comprehension

1. What did Pakhom give the Chief?
   - ☐ **a.** a coat and some tea
   - ☐ **b.** a wooden cart
   - ☐ **c.** 200 rubles

2. The Chief said that Pakhom could have
   - ☐ **a.** a small piece of land.
   - ☐ **b.** all the land that the Chief owned.
   - ☐ **c.** all the land that Pakhom could walk around in a day.

3. The Chief told Pakhom to
   - ☐ **a.** walk as fast as he could.
   - ☐ **b.** walk very slowly.
   - ☐ **c.** dig some holes as he walked.

4. Pakhom dreamed that the traveler was
   - ☐ **a.** riding a horse.
   - ☐ **b.** talking to the Chief.
   - ☐ **c.** laughing loudly.

5. How far did Pakhom think he could walk in a day?
   - ☐ **a.** about 10 miles
   - ☐ **b.** 30 or 35 miles
   - ☐ **c.** 100 miles

6. Pakhom put the 500 rubles
   - ☐ **a.** under a stone.
   - ☐ **b.** on the Chief's hat.
   - ☐ **c.** next to a tree.

7. The helper gave Pakhom
   - ☐ **a.** money.
   - ☐ **b.** bread and water.
   - ☐ **c.** a bottle filled with tea.

Vocabulary

8. Some of the men came near the Chief and whispered in his ear. When you *whisper*, you
   - ☐ **a.** shout very loudly.
   - ☐ **b.** speak very softly.
   - ☐ **c.** watch very closely.

9. The price of the land was 500 rubles a day. The word *price* means
   - ☐ **a.** cost.
   - ☐ **b.** size.
   - ☐ **c.** color.

Idioms

10. The Chief said, "But keep in mind, you must return to this spot before the sun sets!" The idiom *keep in mind* means
    - ☐ **a.** do not forget.
    - ☐ **b.** ask many questions.
    - ☐ **c.** to win.

How many questions did you answer correctly? Circle your score. Then fill in your score on the Score Chart on page 216.

Number Correct	Score
1	10
2	20
3	30
4	40
5	50
6	60
7	70
8	80
9	90
10	100

Understanding the Story

Exercise A ~ Checking Comprehension

Answer each question by writing a complete sentence. Begin each sentence with a capital letter, and end each sentence with a period. You may use the line numbers in parentheses to help you.

1. What was the Chief wearing? (1)

2. What did Pakhom give the Chief? (4)

3. What was the price of the land? (13)

4. What did the Chief give Pakhom? (29)

5. Why couldn't Pakhom sleep that night? (34)

6. When did Pakhom finally fall asleep? (39)

7. What did the Chief put on the ground? (63)

8. What did the helper give Pakhom? (71)

Exercise B ~ Building Sentences

Make sentences by adding the correct letter.

1. ______	Pakhom gave some presents	a.	choose a piece of land.
2. ______	The Chief said Pakhom could	b.	a huge piece of land.
3. ______	Pakhom could have all the land that he	c.	a strange dream.
4. ______	Pakhom thought he would get	d.	walked around in a day.
5. ______	That night Pakhom had	e.	to the Chief.

Now do questions 6–10 the same way.

6. ______	The next morning Pakhom	a.	he wanted to go.
7. ______	They walked until they came	b.	wonderful land.
8. ______	The Bashkirs had	c.	to the top of a hill.
9. ______	Pakhom could walk wherever	d.	the sun set.
10. ______	He had to return before	e.	woke up his helper.

Now write the sentences on the lines below. Remember to begin each sentence with a capital letter and to end each sentence with a period.

1. ______________________________
2. ______________________________
3. ______________________________
4. ______________________________
5. ______________________________
6. ______________________________
7. ______________________________
8. ______________________________
9. ______________________________
10. ______________________________

Exercise C ~ Adding Vocabulary

In the box are 5 words and an idiom from the story. Complete each sentence by adding the correct word.

at once	shovel	fur
rent	pocket	agree

1. The Chief was wearing a large ________________ coat.
2. When the Chief arrived, Pakhom went to the cart ________________.
3. The Chief said, "I ________________ to sell the land to Pakhom."
4. Pakhom had 500 rubles in his ________________.
5. The Chief gave Pakhom a ________________ so that he could dig some holes.
6. He thought he would sell some of the land and ________________ some of it to farmers.

Exercise D ~ Picking a Pronoun

Fill in each blank by adding the correct **possessive pronoun** from the box. Use each pronoun once.

my	yours	his	its	our	their

1. The Chief touched the hat with ________________ foot.
2. He said, "Whatever land you walk around will be ________________."
3. Pakhom thought, "I'll keep the best land for myself. That's where I'll have ________________ farm."
4. The man told Pakhom, "This is ________________ Chief."
5. Pakhom carried the shovel by ________________ handle.
6. The Bashkirs always listened to ________________ Chief.

Exercise E ~ Putting Words in Order

Make sentences by putting the words in the correct order.

1. price / The / was / 500 / day / a / rubles

____

2. sleep / not / night / could / Pakhom / That

____

3. thinking / land / the / Pakhom / about / was

____

4. had / Pakhom / dream / strange / a

____

5. Chief / hat / fur / off / took / The / his

____

6. cart / helper / His / in / the / sleeping / was

____

7. pocket / bread / into / his / put / He

____

8. ground / the / He / on / put / hat / the

____

Exercise F ~ Vocabulary Review

Part A

Write a complete sentence for each word or idiom.

1. fur ______________________________

2. pocket ______________________________

3. shovel ______________________________

4. rent ______________________________

5. agree ______________________________

6. whispered ______________________________

7. price ______________________________

8. keep in mind (idiom) ______________________________

Part B

Write about what happened in the story. Use four or more vocabulary words.

____

Before You Read Part 3

Pakhom can have all the land that he can walk around in a day. The land will cost only 500 rubles. But Pakhom must return to the place he started before the day is over. If Pakhom takes longer than a day, he will lose his money. What do you think will happen? Will Pakhom get a large piece of land, a small piece of land, or will he lose his money? Will something else happen? See if you are right.

PART 3

Pakhom looked around. He wondered where to walk. The land was good everywhere.

Finally he thought, "I will walk toward the east." He turned toward the east and waited for the sun to rise.

Soon Pakhom saw the first light of the sun. He walked down the hill and marched on to the plain.

Pakhom walked quickly. He carried the shovel over his shoulder. After he had walked about a mile, Pakhom stopped. "This is where I will dig the first hole," he thought. Pakhom dug the hole and put the little pile of earth next to it. "That will make the hole easier to see," he said. He walked on for a while. Then he dug another hole.

Pakhom looked back. He could see the hill with the people on it. He guessed that he had walked three miles. It was getting warmer. He took off his coat and threw it over his shoulder. Then he walked until he stopped to dig another hole.

It was getting very warm. Pakhom looked at the sun and felt a little tired. "I will take off my heavy boots," he said. "That will make it easier to walk." Pakhom sat down and took off his boots. Then he stood up and began to walk. It was easier to walk without his boots.

"I will walk for another three miles," he thought. "Then I will turn to the left. The land here is very good. I don't want to give it up."

Pakhom walked for a long time. Then he turned around and looked toward the hill. It was far away. The people on the hill looked very small.

Pakhom thought, "I have gone far enough in this direction. I must stop here and turn to the left. Anyway, I am very thirsty."

Pakhom stopped. He dug a hole and took a drink of water. Then he turned to the left and went on.

By now Pakhom was very tired. He looked at the sun and saw that it was noon. "I must stop and rest," he said.

Pakhom sat down on the ground. He ate some bread and drank

some water. Then he went on again. The food made him feel better. But he was very hot. He also felt sleepy.

Pakhom walked for a long time. He was going to turn to the left. But he looked at the land ahead of him. It was very good land. "I must have that piece of land," he thought. So he walked on.

Pakhom went about a mile. Then he dug a hole and turned to the left. Now he looked toward the hill. It seemed very, very far away. It was so far away that it was hard for him to see it. He looked at the sun. It was just beginning to set.

Pakhom thought, "I must hurry back **right now**! I must go back at once! Perhaps I went too far! Anyhow, I have a big piece of land."

Pakhom headed toward the hill, but it was hard to walk. His feet were cut and his legs felt weak. He wanted to rest, but that was not possible. He *had* to get back before the sun set! And the sun was going down.

"Oh, dear," thought Pakhom, "did I go too far? Can I get back in time? What if I am too late?"

Pakhom looked at the hill. Then he looked at the sun. He was still far from the hill—and the sun was almost down!

It was very hard to walk, but he went faster and faster. He hurried on. But he was still far from the hill.

Pakhom began to run. He threw away the water and the bread, but he kept the shovel. He **leaned** against it while he ran.

"What shall I do?" he thought. "I was **greedy** and went too far. What if I can't get back before the sun sets?"

His mouth was very dry. And now his heart was beating like a hammer. It was pounding very loudly. Still he went on. He could not stop.

"I can't stop now!" he thought. "They will call me a fool if I stop now! I have run very far. I can't stop now!"

He ran on and on. Then he heard the Bashkirs. They were yelling at him. They were cheering. They were shouting at him to keep running. Pakhom heard them. He kept running.

The sun was almost down. Yes, the sun was about to set. It was very low in the sky. But Pakhom was very near the hill! He could see the people on the hill! They were waving their arms at him. They were shouting at him to hurry.

Pakhom could see the spot where he started. He could see the fur hat on the ground. He could see the rubles on the hat. And he could see the Chief! The Chief was sitting on the ground. He seemed to be smiling. Then Pakhom remembered his dream. He wondered if he would get the land.

Pakhom looked at the sun. It was almost down! It was nearly touching the ground! He rushed on.

Just as he reached the hill, it suddenly got dark. Pakhom looked up. He saw that the sun had set! He cried out, "I have lost everything!"

Pakhom stopped running. But then he heard the Bashkirs. They were still shouting. They were yelling at him to hurry. Then Pakhom remembered that they were on top of the hill. He was at the bottom. They could still see the sun!

He took a deep breath and ran up the hill. It was still light there! Pakhom reached the top. He saw the fur hat! He saw the Chief! The Chief was still smiling. Again Pakhom remembered his dream.

Pakhom cried out, "Ahhhh!" As he fell forward, his fingers touched the hat.

"Well done!" cried the Chief. "Much land is yours!"

Pakhom's helper ran to him. He tried to help Pakhom get up. But Pakhom did not move. Blood was flowing from his mouth. Pakhom was dead!

The Bashkirs shook their heads sadly.

The helper took the shovel and dug a grave. A little piece of land was all that he needed. It was just big enough for Pakhom to lie in. It was six feet long from his head to his toes.

Meet the Author

Leo Tolstoy (1828–1910) was one of Russia's greatest writers. Most of his books and stories are about the meaning of life. Tolstoy believed that people should try to do good things and help one another. He lived his life that way. He gave away his land and most of his money. When he died, he was a poor man. You can see some of Tolstoy's ideas in "Land." His most famous books are *War and Peace* and *Anna Karenina*.

Check Your Reading

Put an **X** in the box next to the correct answer.

How many questions did you answer correctly? Circle your score. Then fill in your score on the Score Chart on page 216.

Number Correct	Score
1	10
2	20
3	30
4	40
5	50
6	60
7	70
8	80
9	90
10	100

Reading Comprehension

1. Pakhom began to walk toward the
   - ☐ **a.** west.
   - ☐ **b.** east.
   - ☐ **c.** south.

2. As Pakhom walked along, he
   - ☐ **a.** dug holes.
   - ☐ **b.** sang songs.
   - ☐ **c.** shouted at the Bashkirs.

3. Pakhom threw away
   - ☐ **a.** the shovel.
   - ☐ **b.** the water and the bread.
   - ☐ **c.** his belt.

4. It was hard for Pakhom to walk at the end because
   - ☐ **a.** the land was covered with rocks.
   - ☐ **b.** he didn't know where he was going.
   - ☐ **c.** his feet were cut and his legs felt weak.

5. Pakhom began to hurry back when he
   - ☐ **a.** looked at his watch and saw that it was late.
   - ☐ **b.** heard the Chief calling him.
   - ☐ **c.** saw that the sun was beginning to set.

6. Pakhom thought the Chief was
   - ☐ **a.** smiling.
   - ☐ **b.** crying.
   - ☐ **c.** shaking his head sadly.

Vocabulary

7. As he ran, Pakhom leaned against the shovel. The word *leaned* means
   - ☐ **a.** rested against.
   - ☐ **b.** yelled at.
   - ☐ **c.** broke into pieces.

8. Pakhom said, "I was greedy and went too far." Someone who is *greedy*
   - ☐ **a.** wants very little.
   - ☐ **b.** wants too much.
   - ☐ **c.** gives things away.

9. The helper dug a grave for Pakhom. A *grave* is a
   - ☐ **a.** small wooden box.
   - ☐ **b.** small garden.
   - ☐ **c.** hole in the ground for a dead body.

Idioms

10. When it got late Pakhom said, "I must hurry back right now!" The idiom *right now* means
    - ☐ **a.** at once.
    - ☐ **b.** in an hour.
    - ☐ **c.** later.

UNDERSTANDING THE STORY

Exercise A ~ Checking Comprehension

Answer each question by writing a complete sentence. Begin each sentence with a capital letter, and end each sentence with a period. You may use the line numbers in parentheses to help you.

1. Which way did Pakhom walk? (3)

2. Why did Pakhom take off his boots? (17)

3. Why was it hard for him to walk at the end? (43)

4. Why did Pakhom have to hurry back? (46)

5. What did Pakhom throw away? (53)

6. What were the Bashkirs shouting at Pakhom? (63)

7. When he saw the Chief smiling, what did Pakhom remember? (72)

8. After Pakhom fell, why didn't he move? (89)

9. What did the helper dig? (92)

10. How big was Pakhom's grave? (94)

Exercise B ~ Building Sentences

Build sentences by adding the correct letter.

1. _____	Pakhom carried the shovel over	**a.**	was beginning to set.
2. _____	He walked for a mile and	**b.**	his shoulder.
3. _____	Pakhom turned and looked back	**c.**	looked very small.
4. _____	The people on the hill	**d.**	then dug the first hole.
5. _____	Pakhom saw that the sun	**e.**	toward the hill.

Now do questions 6–10 the same way.

6. _____	Pakhom began to	**a.**	yelling at him to hurry.
7. _____	His heart was beating	**b.**	run back to the hill.
8. _____	He heard the Bashkirs	**c.**	touched the hat.
9. _____	Finally his fingers	**d.**	he was dead.
10. _____	Pakhom did not move because	**e.**	very loudly.

Now write the sentences on the lines below. Remember to begin each sentence with a capital letter and to end each sentence with a period.

1. ______________________________

2. ______________________________

3. ______________________________

4. ______________________________

5. ______________________________

6. ______________________________

7. ______________________________

8. ______________________________

9. ______________________________

10. ______________________________

Exercise C ~ Adding Vocabulary

In the box are 8 words from the story. Complete each sentence by adding the correct word.

marched	boots	pile	rise
direction	flowing	waving	possible

1. Pakhom turned to the east and waited for the sun to ________________.
2. He walked down the hill and ________________ on to the plain.
3. He put the little ________________ of earth next to the hole.
4. His heavy ________________ made it hard to walk.
5. Pakhom said, "I have gone far enough in this ________________."
6. The Bashkirs were ________________ their arms at him.
7. Pakhom wanted to rest but that was not ________________.
8. Blood was ________________ from his mouth.

Exercise D ~ Using Verbs Correctly

Fill in each blank by writing *Present, Past,* or *Future* to show the tense of the verb in each sentence. The first one has been done for you.

1. Pakhom looked around. *Past*
2. I will walk to the east. ________________
3. Pakhom dug another hole. ________________
4. I am very tired. ________________
5. He will sell some of the land. ________________
6. Pakhom went too far. ________________
7. The hill is far away. ________________
8. He sees the fur hat. ________________

Exercise E ~ Changing Statements to Questions

Change each statement to a question. Begin each question with the word or words in parentheses. Put a question mark at the end of each question. The first one has been done for you.

1. Pakhom saw the hill. (What)

   What did Pakhom see?

2. The food made him feel better. (What)

3. His heart was beating loudly. (How)

4. Pakhom walked for three miles. (How far)

5. Pakhom ate some bread. (What)

6. Pakhom was very near the hill. (Where)

7. Pakhom saw the Chief. (Who)

8. Pakhom remembered his dream. (What)

9. They could see the sun because they were on top of the hill. (Why)

10. A little piece of land was all that the helper needed. (How much)

Exercise F ~ Vocabulary Review

Part A

Write a complete sentence for each word or idiom.

1. rise ______________________________

2. marched ______________________________

3. direction ______________________________

4. waving ______________________________

5. possible ______________________________

6. greedy ______________________________

7. grave ______________________________

8. right now (idiom) ______________________________

Part B

Write about what happened in the story. Use four or more vocabulary words.

Studying the Story

A. Looking Back at the Story

Discuss these questions with your partner or with the group. Your teacher may ask you to write your answer to one or more of the questions.

- The Chief told Pakhom that the price of the land was 500 rubles a day. Explain what the Chief meant. Why was Pakhom surprised?
- In Pakhom's dream, the Chief and the traveler laughed at him. What does this mean?
- What killed Pakhom? Explain your answer.
- At the end of the story, how big was the piece of land that Pakhom got? Why do you think Tolstoy ended the story this way? What is he telling the reader?

B. Using a Chart to Gather Information

Suppose that Pakhom had not died. Suppose that he returned to his old farm. What do you think he would tell his neighbors about the Bashkirs? Write one fact about the Bashkirs in each box in the **cluster map** below. One fact has already been added. You may look back at the story.

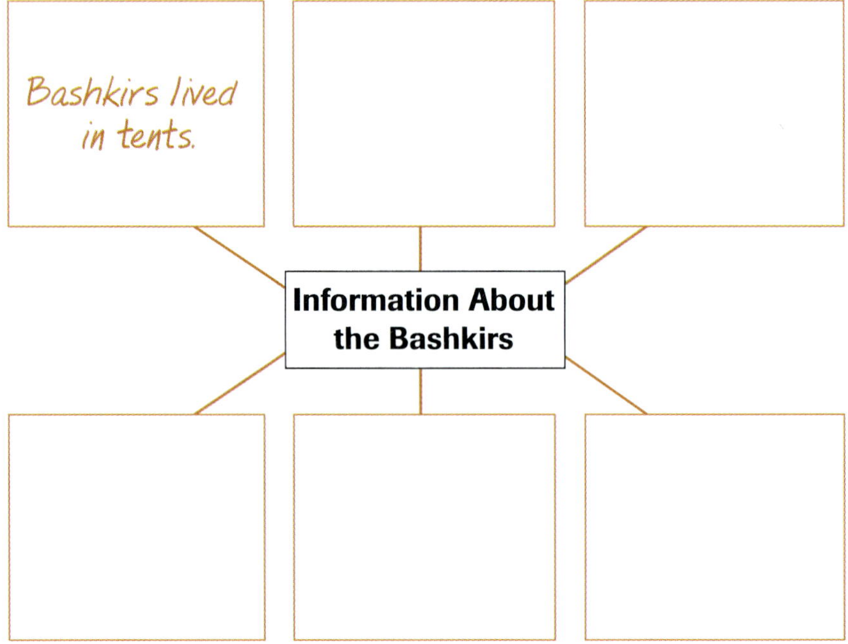

Thinking About Literature

1. Here is your chance to be a character in a story. Suppose that you were the Chief of the Bashkirs. What would you tell a stranger about Pakhom? Complete the paragraph below.

   One day a man named Pakhom came to our land.

2. Answer each question in a complete sentence.

   a. What was Pakhom's motive for giving the Bashkirs many gifts?

   b. What was Pakhom's motive for walking so far in the land of the Bashkirs?

   c. At the end of the story, the people shouted at Pakhom and waved their arms. What was their motive for yelling at him to hurry?

   d. Why do you think Tolstoy wrote this story? What was his motive?

UNIT 6

MRS. PENN'S STORY

BY MARY WILKINS FREEMAN

GETTING READY TO READ

1. The Story and You

In this story, you will meet Sarah and Adam Penn. Mr. Penn wants to build a barn, but his wife does not want him to build one. Think of a time when you wanted to do something, and someone tried to stop you from doing it. How did you handle the problem? Tell what happened.

2. Learning About Literature

Look at **The Story and You**. As you can see, Mr. Penn wants to build a barn, but his wife does not want him to build one. There is **conflict** between the two people. Conflict takes place when characters in a story do not agree. Each character has a different "point of view"—or way of looking at something. Sometimes, the characters struggle. They may even fight. As you might expect, conflict can make a story very exciting.

3. Looking Ahead

Look at the picture on the left. Think about the title of the story. Who do you think the two people standing next to the fence are? Do you think they live in the country or in the city? How do you think they earn a living? What details in the picture helped you answer these questions? Read on to see if you are right.

Mrs. Penn's Story

by Mary Wilkins Freeman

Part 1

"Father!"

"What is it?"

"Look over there. Why are those men digging in that field?"

The old man was patting a horse and did not look up. He did not answer.

"Father!"

The man kept patting the horse.

"Look here, father. I want to know why those men are digging in that field over there. I want to know, and I'm going to know."

The old man looked at her. "I wish you would go into the house, mother," he said. "You have work to do."

But the woman stood there waiting. She was a small woman with light gray hair. Her name was Sarah Penn. Her husband's name was Adam. But she always called him *father*. And he addressed her as *mother*.

They were standing in the barn. The doors were wide open, and the spring air was full of the smell of growing grass.

The old man glanced at his wife. She stared back at him, solid as a rock. He slapped the horse one more time and began to leave.

"Father!" she **demanded**.

The man stopped. "What is it?"

"I want to know why those men are digging over there. And I'm going **to find out**."

"Well, if you have to know, I'll tell you. They're digging a cellar, I guess."

"A cellar for what?"

"A barn."

"A barn! You're not going to build a barn over there. You said that's where we were going to have a new house."

The man did not say another word. He hurried out of the barn.

The woman stood and watched him for a moment. Then she left

the barn and walked across to the house. The house stood near the barn and some other farm buildings. But the house was the smallest building of them all.

A pretty girl was looking out of one of the windows in the house. She was watching the workers who were digging in the field. She turned when her mother entered the room.

"Mother," she asked, "what are they digging for? Did he tell you?"

"They're digging for—for a cellar for a new barn."

"For another barn?" she said.

"That's what he says."

A boy stood in front of the mirror in the kitchen. He was combing his hair. He did not seem to be listening to them.

"Sammy," said the girl, "did you know that father was going to build a new barn?"

The boy waited a few moments before answering. "Yes, I guess I did," he finally said.

"Why didn't you tell me about it?" asked Mrs. Penn.

"I didn't think it would do any good," he answered.

"I don't know why father wants another barn," said the girl.

Mrs. Penn asked her son, "Is he going to buy more cows?"

"I suppose so," said the boy.

The boy got his cap, took some books from a shelf, and started for school. Mother and daughter went to the sink that was filled with dishes. "Mother," said the girl, "it's too bad that father is going to build a new barn. What we need is a more **modern** house."

Sarah Penn washed a dish fiercely. She said, "You haven't found out that we're women-folks, Nancy. One of these days, you'll find it out. You shouldn't judge your father, though. He just doesn't look at things the way we do. And we've been pretty comfortable here after all. Nobody ever heard me complain."

Sarah Penn finished the dishes. Then she swept the house. She was thinking about her daughter, Nancy, who was going to be married in the fall. Mrs. Penn looked out the window and noticed the men digging. The sight of them digging bothered her greatly.

They were digging the cellar of the new barn—in the place where, forty years ago, Adam had promised her that their new house would stand.

Later that day, Mrs. Penn spoke to Adam. "Father!" she called.

"Well, what is it?"

"I want to see you for just a minute."

"I've got to unload this wood. I can't stop now."

"Father! You come here!"

Sarah Penn stood in the door like a queen. She held her head high, as though she wore a crown. Adam went.

Mrs. Penn led the way into the kitchen. "Sit down, father," she said.

He sat down heavily. "Well, what is it, mother?"

"I want to know why you're building that new barn, father. Are you going to buy more cows?"

Adam did not reply. He shut his mouth tightly.

Sarah Penn stood in front of her husband. "I'm going to talk plainly to you. I never have since I married you, but I'm going to now. I've never complained, and I'm not going to complain now. But I'm going to talk plainly. You see this room here, father. You look at it well. There's no carpet on the floor, and the wallpaper is all dirty and dropping off the walls. We haven't had new wallpaper on the walls for ten years, and then I put it on myself. Our daughter, Nancy, has to have her friends here, and all of them have better than this. And their fathers don't have half your means. It's the room she will have to be married in. We were married in a room with a carpet on the floor! And this is the room my daughter will have to be married in. Look here, father!"

Sarah Penn walked across the room. She **flung** open the door to a tiny bedroom. It was just big enough for a bed and a dresser. "There, father," she said. "That's the room I've had to sleep in for forty years."

Sarah Penn threw open another door. "There's not a better girl in town than our Nancy, and that's the place she has to sleep in. It's not as good as your horse's stall. It's not as warm and tight."

Sarah Penn stood before her husband. "Forty years ago, you promised me that we would have a new house built in the field over there. You've built sheds, and two barns, and now you're going to build another barn. You're **lodging** your animals better than your wife and children. I want to know if you think that's right."

But Adam only answered, "I don't have anything to say."

Check Your Reading

Put an **X** in the box next to the correct answer.

Reading Comprehension

1. Sarah Penn saw some men
   - ☐ **a.** unloading wood.
   - ☐ **b.** digging in a field.
   - ☐ **c.** standing in the barn.

2. Adam Penn planned to
   - ☐ **a.** build a new barn.
   - ☐ **b.** build a new house.
   - ☐ **c.** buy more horses.

3. Nancy was going to be married
   - ☐ **a.** in the fall.
   - ☐ **b.** in the spring.
   - ☐ **c.** in the summer.

4. Sarah Penn's bedroom was
   - ☐ **a.** large.
   - ☐ **b.** tiny.
   - ☐ **c.** beautiful.

5. Mr. And Mrs. Penn had lived in the house
   - ☐ **a.** for nearly twenty years.
   - ☐ **b.** for about fifty years.
   - ☐ **c.** for forty years.

Vocabulary

6. Sarah demanded that Adam listen to her. The word *demanded* means
   - ☐ **a.** asked for strongly.
   - ☐ **b.** cared about.
   - ☐ **c.** hoped for.

7. Nancy said they needed a modern house. Something that is *modern* is
   - ☐ **a.** huge.
   - ☐ **b.** made of wood.
   - ☐ **c.** quite new.

8. She flung open the bedroom door. The word *flung* means
   - ☐ **a.** threw.
   - ☐ **b.** touched.
   - ☐ **c.** hit.

9. Adam was lodging his animals better than his family. As used here, *lodging* means
   - ☐ **a.** giving help.
   - ☐ **b.** giving food.
   - ☐ **c.** giving a place to live.

Idioms

10. Sarah wanted to find out why the men were digging in the field. The idiom *to find out* means
    - ☐ **a.** to give help.
    - ☐ **b.** to know or to learn.
    - ☐ **c.** to send home.

How many questions did you answer correctly? Circle your score. Then fill in your score on the Score Chart on page 216.

Number Correct	Score
1	10
2	20
3	30
4	40
5	50
6	60
7	70
8	80
9	90
10	100

Understanding the Story

Exercise A ~ Checking Comprehension

Answer each question by writing a complete sentence. Begin each sentence with a capital letter, and end each sentence with a period. You may use the line numbers in parentheses to help you.

1. What did Sarah Penn look like? (12)

2. What did Sarah Penn always call her husband? (14)

3. What did Adam Penn always call Sarah? (14)

4. Where did the house stand? (31)

5. What was the boy combing? (41)

6. What did the boy take from a shelf? (52)

7. What was the sink filled with? (53)

8. When was Nancy going to be married? (62)

9. What did the wallpaper look like? (83)

10. How big was Sarah Penn's bedroom? (92)

Exercise B ~ Building Sentences

Make sentences by adding the correct letter.

1. ______ Sarah Penn looked
2. ______ Some men were
3. ______ Adam already had
4. ______ The men were digging
5. ______ She thought the family

a. digging in the field.
b. a cellar for a new barn.
c. needed a new house
d. out of the window.
e. barns and some sheds.

Now do questions 6–10 the same way.

6. ______ Nancy was going
7. ______ Adam Penn had more money
8. ______ Sarah wanted Nancy to be married
9. ______ She did not think
10. ______ Adam did not want to

a. than most of the farmers.
b. to be married soon.
c. talk about it.
d. in a nice house.
e. they needed a new barn.

Now write the sentences on the lines below. Remember to begin each sentence with a capital letter and to end each sentence with a period.

1. ______________________________
2. ______________________________
3. ______________________________
4. ______________________________
5. ______________________________
6. ______________________________
7. ______________________________
8. ______________________________
9. ______________________________
10. ______________________________

Exercise C ~ Adding Vocabulary

In the box are 6 words from the story. Complete each sentence by adding the correct word.

complain	crown	promised
glanced	fiercely	stall

1. Adam ________________ at his wife. He saw that she was staring at him.
2. Many years ago, he ________________ to build a new house in the field.
3. Although she did not ________________ to Adam, Sarah told him what she thought.
4. Sarah seemed angry. She began to wash a dish ________________.
5. He kept his horses in a ________________ that was "warm and tight."
6. Sarah held her head high, as though she wore a ________________ on her head.

Exercise D ~ Picking Adjectives and Adverbs

Fill in each blank by adding the correct adjective or adverb from the box. Use each word once. Circle *adjective* or *adverb* to show what you added.

quickly	small	hard	softly	old

1. Sarah Penn was a ________________ woman with gray hair.
   (adjective, adverb)
2. She left the barn and walked ________________ to the house.
   (adjective, adverb)
3. Nancy never raised her voice. She always spoke ________________.
   (adjective, adverb)
4. The ________________ wallpaper was dropping off the walls.
   (adjective, adverb)
5. Adam was a farmer. He was used to doing ________________ work.
   (adjective, adverb)

Exercise E ~ Using Verbs Correctly

Fill in each blank using the **past tense** of the **irregular verb** in parentheses.

1. Sarah Penn ____________________ some men who were digging in a field. (see)
2. Sarah ____________________ to Adam about the men. (speak).
3. Adam Penn ____________________ not answer for a long time. (do)
4. He just ____________________ there without speaking. (stand)
5. Finally, Adam ____________________ that the men were digging a cellar. (say)
6. Sarah ____________________ into the old house. (go)
7. She ____________________ her daughter, Nancy, in the kitchen. (meet)
8. Sammy ____________________ that his father was going to build a new barn. (hear).
9. Later, Sarah Penn ____________________ Adam. (find)
10. She ____________________ Adam into the kitchen. (bring)
11. Sarah ____________________ Adam through the house. (take)
12. Sarah ____________________ to talk about the old house. (begin)
13. They ____________________ many things in the house a long time ago. (buy)
14. She said that Adam ____________________ more money than the other farmers. (have)
15. Sarah ____________________ Adam they needed a new house. (tell).

Exercise F ~ Vocabulary Review

Part A

Write a complete sentence for each word.

1. glanced ______________________________
2. promised ______________________________
3. stall ______________________________
4. modern ______________________________
5. fiercely ______________________________
6. complain ______________________________
7. crown ______________________________
8. to find out (idiom) ______________________________

Part B

Write about what happened in the story. Use three or more of the vocabulary words and an idiom.

Before You Read Part 2

Forty years ago, Adam promised his wife that he would build her a house. He never built that house. Now he is building another barn. Mrs. Penn is very unhappy about that. Do you think she will get her new house? See if you are right.

PART 2

Adam planned to move his cows into the new barn on Wednesday. On Tuesday morning, he received a letter that changed his plans.

He told his wife, "I just got a letter from Hiram." Hiram was his brother who lived in Vermont. "He says if I come *now*, I can buy just the kind of horse I want. I hate to leave, but I guess I should go."

Adam's voice became unusually soft. "Look, mother," he said, "when the new cows arrive, Sammy can drive them into the new barn. He can handle them **for the time being**."

Adam walked to the door. He seemed a bit nervous. "I should be back by Saturday night," he told Sarah Penn.

"Do be careful," said his wife.

Mrs. Penn worked all morning. But she kept thinking about the letter from Hiram. "It's strange that it should come just now," she said to herself. "It seems like a sign." She kept thinking about the letter. And then, finally, she decided what to do.

During lunch, Mrs. Penn turned to Sammy and Nancy. "Let me know when you have finished eating," she said. "I want you to help me."

Nancy and Sammy stared at each other. There was something strange in their mother's manner. Mrs. Penn did not eat anything herself. She went to a closet, and the children heard her moving dishes. Soon she came back with a pile of plates. She took out a basket and filled it with the dishes.

"What are you doing, mother?" asked Nancy in a low voice.

"You'll see what I am going to do," said Mrs. Penn. "If you are through, Nancy, I want you to pack up your things. And, Sammy, I want you to help me take down the bed in the bedroom."

"Oh, mother, what for?" gasped Nancy.

"You'll see," said her mother.

During the next few hours, the whole family worked. By five o'clock, the little house was empty. Everything had been moved into the new barn.

Mrs. Penn walked around in the new barn. She was very pleased with what she saw. Those large stalls would make wonderful bedrooms. They would be better than the one that she had lived in for forty years. There was a perfect space for a kitchen—one fit for a palace. A little work was needed, but with some walls and windows, what a house it would be!

At six o'clock, the kettle was boiling and the table was set for their dinner. The barn looked like a new home.

The next day, Adam's new cows arrived. Sarah ordered them to be put in the old barn. Then the family waited for Adam.

On Saturday, Sammy looked out of the window of the new barn. "There he is!" Sammy announced.

Mrs. Penn kept on working. The children watched Adam. He left the new horse standing in the road. Then he went to the house door. It was locked. Adam turned slowly around. He seemed a little **puzzled**.

Adam led his new horse across the yard to the new barn. The barn doors rolled open. There stood his family!

"Why are you all down here?" said Adam. "What is the matter at the house?"

"We've come here to live, father," said Sammy. His thin voice trembled bravely.

"What's this?" Adam **sniffed** something. "It smells like cooking." He stepped forward and looked in the barn. Then he turned to his wife. His face was pale and frightened. "What on earth does this mean, mother?" he gasped.

"You come in here, father," said Sarah Penn. She led him into the house and shut the door. "Now, father," she said. "There is no reason to be scared. I'm not crazy and nothing is wrong. But we've come to live here, and we're going to live here. We have just as much right to be here as horses and cows. The house wasn't fit for us to live in any longer, and I decided I wasn't going to stay there any more. I've been at your side for forty years, and I'll be there now. But I'm going to live here. You'll have to put in some windows and walls. And you'll have to buy some **furniture**."

"Why, mother!" Adam gasped.

"You better take off your coat and get washed. And then we'll have dinner."

"Why, mother."

Adam shook his head. He could hardly speak. He tried to take off his coat, but his arms seemed to **lack** the power. His wife helped him.

He looked at the meal on the table. He could hardly believe it. The kitchen looked so beautiful, and the food looked so good.

"Excuse me," said Adam. He stumbled outside and sat down on the steps. Sarah joined him a moment later. It was beginning to get dark. There was a clear, dark blue glow in the sky. Before them stretched the fields. The air was cool and calm and sweet.

Sarah bent over. She touched her husband on one of his shoulders. "Father!"

The old man's shoulders were moving. He was weeping.

"Why, father, don't," said Sarah.

"I'll put in windows—doors—everything you want."

Adam was like a great fort whose walls had come tumbling down.

"Why, mother," he said, his voice cracking, "I had no idea this meant so much to you."

Meet the Author

Mary Wilkins Freeman (1852–1930) wrote about life in New England. That is the northeastern part of the United States. Freeman lived most of her life in Massachusetts and Vermont. She knew a lot about the people who lived in that area. Freeman wrote nearly 250 stories. She also wrote 12 books and a play. But she is remembered for her short stories. Sarah Penn is her most famous character.

Check Your Reading

Put an **X** in the box next to the correct answer.

How many questions did you answer correctly? Circle your score. Then fill in your score on the Score Chart on page 216.

Number Correct	Score
1	10
2	20
3	30
4	40
5	50
6	60
7	70
8	80
9	90
10	100

Reading Comprehension

1. Adam got a letter from his brother on
   - ☐ **a.** Tuesday.
   - ☐ **b.** Wednesday.
   - ☐ **c.** Saturday.

2. Mr. Penn went to Vermont to
   - ☐ **a.** buy some cows.
   - ☐ **b.** buy a horse.
   - ☐ **c.** visit his sick brother.

3. Sammy and Nancy helped their mother
   - ☐ **a.** feed the new cows.
   - ☐ **b.** make lunch.
   - ☐ **c.** move everything into the new barn.

4. When Adam saw his family in the new barn, he
   - ☐ **a.** turned pale and became frightened.
   - ☐ **b.** told them they were crazy.
   - ☐ **c.** started to laugh.

5. At the end of the story, Adam
   - ☐ **a.** got angry at Sarah.
   - ☐ **b.** went back to the old house.
   - ☐ **c.** began to weep.

Vocabulary

6. When Adam saw that the front door was locked, he seemed a little puzzled. When you are *puzzled*, you
   - ☐ **a.** are happy.
   - ☐ **b.** feel lonely.
   - ☐ **c.** don't know what to do.

7. Adam sniffed something cooking. As used here, the word *sniffed* means
   - ☐ **a.** smelled.
   - ☐ **b.** ate.
   - ☐ **c.** listened.

8. Sarah said that Adam would have to buy some furniture for the house. The word *furniture* means
   - ☐ **a.** windows and walls.
   - ☐ **b.** chairs, tables, and beds.
   - ☐ **c.** a new roof.

9. He felt weak, and he seemed to lack the power to take off his coat. The word *lack* means
   - ☐ **a.** to look everywhere.
   - ☐ **b.** to not have enough.
   - ☐ **c.** to be surprised.

Idioms

10. Sammy could handle the cows for the time being. The idiom *for the time being* means
    - ☐ **a.** after a while.
    - ☐ **b.** in a week.
    - ☐ **c.** for now.

Understanding the Story

Exercise A ~ Checking Comprehension

Answer each question by writing a complete sentence. Begin each sentence with a capital letter, and end each sentence with a period. You may use the line numbers in parentheses to help you.

1. When did Adam receive a letter? (2)

2. Who was Hiram? (4)

3. When did Adam think he would be back? (11)

4. What did Mrs. Penn keep thinking about? (13)

5. Where had everything been moved? (32)

6. When did Adam's new cows arrive? (42)

7. What did Adam discover when he went to the house door? (47)

8. What had Sarah decided? (64)

9. Where did Adam sit? (77)

10. Why were the old man's shoulders moving? (83)

Exercise B ~ Building Sentences

Make sentences by adding the correct letter.

1. ______ Adam planned to put his
2. ______ A letter from Hiram
3. ______ Suddenly, Adam had to
4. ______ The family moved everything into
5. ______ Sarah was pleased with

a. go to Vermont.
b. the way everything looked.
c. the new barn.
d. changed Adam's plans.
e. cows into the new barn.

Now do questions 6–10 the same way.

6. ______ Adam returned and went to
7. ______ He discovered that the
8. ______ He found his family
9. ______ Sarah said that they
10. ______ Adam did not know

a. door was locked.
b. were going to live there.
c. it meant so much to Sarah.
d. in the new barn.
e. the front door.

Now write the sentences on the lines below. Remember to begin each sentence with a capital letter, and to end each sentence with a period.

1. ______________________________
2. ______________________________
3. ______________________________
4. ______________________________
5. ______________________________
6. ______________________________
7. ______________________________
8. ______________________________
9. ______________________________
10. ______________________________

Exercise C ~ Adding Vocabulary

In the box are 8 words from the story. Complete each sentence by adding the correct word. Use each word once.

palace	stumbled	nervous	shoulders
announced	perfect	manner	boiling

1. Adam's voice was soft, and he seemed to be ________________.
2. Nancy and Sammy looked at each other. There was something strange in their mother's ________________.
3. Sarah thought that the new barn would be a ________________ house for the family.
4. The beautiful kitchen was fit for a ________________.
5. The kettle was ________________, and the table was set for their dinner.
6. "There he is!" ________________ Sammy.
7. Adam was very surprised. He ________________ outside and sat down.
8. Sarah touched her husband on one of his ________________.

Exercise D ~ Changing Statements to Questions

Change each statement to a question. Begin each statement with the word or words in parentheses. Put a question mark at the end of each question. The first one has been done for you.

1. Hiram sent a letter from Vermont. (Who)

   Who sent a letter from Vermont?

2. Mrs. Penn worked all morning. (How long)

   ____

3. During lunch, Sarah asked her children to help her. (When)

   ____

4. For the next few hours, the whole family worked. (How long)

   ____

5. By five o'clock, the little house was empty. (When)

   ____

6. Adam went to the front door of the house. (Where)

   ____

7. Mr. Penn was surprised because the front door was locked. (Why)

   ____

8. The house needed windows and walls. (What)

   ____

9. The kitchen looked beautiful. (How)

   ____

10. Adam started to weep because he was filled with emotion. (Why)

    ____

Exercise E ~ True or False?

Part A

Write **T** if the sentence is true. Write **F** if the sentence is false. You may look back at the story.

1. ________ Adam Penn went to Vermont to buy a cow.
2. ________ While Mrs. Penn worked, she kept thinking about the letter.
3. ________ The family moved everything into the new barn.
4. ________ Sammy helped his mother put the new bed in the bedroom.
5. ________ Mrs. Penn was not pleased with her new kitchen.
6. ________ Adam returned home on Thursday.
7. ________ When Mr. Penn returned to the old house, he found it was locked.
8. ________ When Adam saw his family in the new barn, he was very surprised.
9. ________ Mr. Penn went outside and sat down on a chair.
10. ________ At the end of the story, Adam began to smile.

Part B

On the lines below, correct the five false sentences.

1. ____
2. ____
3. ____
4. ____
5. ____

Exercise F ~ Vocabulary Review

Part A

Write a complete sentence for each word.

1. perfect ______________________________
____
2. boiling ______________________________
____
3. stumbled ______________________________
____
4. puzzled ______________________________
____
5. nervous ______________________________
____
6. shoulders ______________________________
____
7. palace ______________________________
____
8. announced ______________________________
____

Part B

Write about what happened in the story. Use four or more of the vocabulary words above.

____
____
____
____
____
____
____

Studying the Story

A. Looking Back at the Story

Discuss these questions with your partner or with the group. Your teacher may ask you to write your answer to one or more of the questions.

- What happened at the beginning of the story that made Mrs. Penn unhappy?
- Why did Adam have to leave suddenly to go to Vermont?
- Do you think that Sarah did the right thing when she moved the family into the new barn? Explain your answer.
- When Adam returned home, he discovered that the door to the house was locked. How did Adam feel then? How did he feel at the end of the story? How do you know?

B. Using a Chart to Show How Characters Change

Sometimes, characters in a story change. When this happens, it is called **character development**. Use the chart below to list the changes in Sarah and Adam during the story.

Changes in Sarah and Adam	
Sarah at Beginning of Story	Sarah at End of Story
Adam at Beginning of Story	Adam at End of Story

Thinking About Literature

1. Pretend that you are Adam Penn. Explain why you want to build a new barn. Tell why you think Sarah does not need a new house. Give as many reasons as you can.

2. Now pretend that you are Sarah Penn. Explain why you need a new house. Give as many reasons as you can.

3. Which person—Adam or Sarah—do you think is "right"? Explain your answer.

Irregular Verbs

Present Tense	Past Tense	Past Participle
be (am/is/are)	was/were	began
begin	began	begun
blow	blew	blown
break	broke	broken
bring	brought	brought
buy	bought	bought
come	came	come
dig	dug	dug
do	did	done
draw	drew	drawn
drink	drank	drunk
eat	ate	eaten
fall	fell	fallen
feel	felt	felt
find	found	found
fly	flew	flown
get	got	gotten
go	went	gone
grow	grew	grown
have	had	had
hear	heard	heard
lead	led	led
make	made	made
meet	met	met
ride	rode	ridden
run	ran	run

Present Tense	Past Tense	Past Participle
say	said	said
see	saw	seen
sell	sold	sold
shake	shook	shaken
sit	sat	sat
speak	spoke	spoken
stand	stood	stood
strike	struck	struck
take	took	taken
tell	told	told
think	thought	thought
throw	threw	thrown
wake	woke or waked	woken or waked
write	wrote	written

Score Chart

This is the Score Chart for **CHECK YOUR READING**. Shade in your score for each part of the story. For example, if your score was 80 for Part 1 of **Wolf**, look at the bottom of the chart for Part 1, **Wolf**. Then shade in the bar up to 80. By looking at this chart, you can see how well you did on each part of the story.

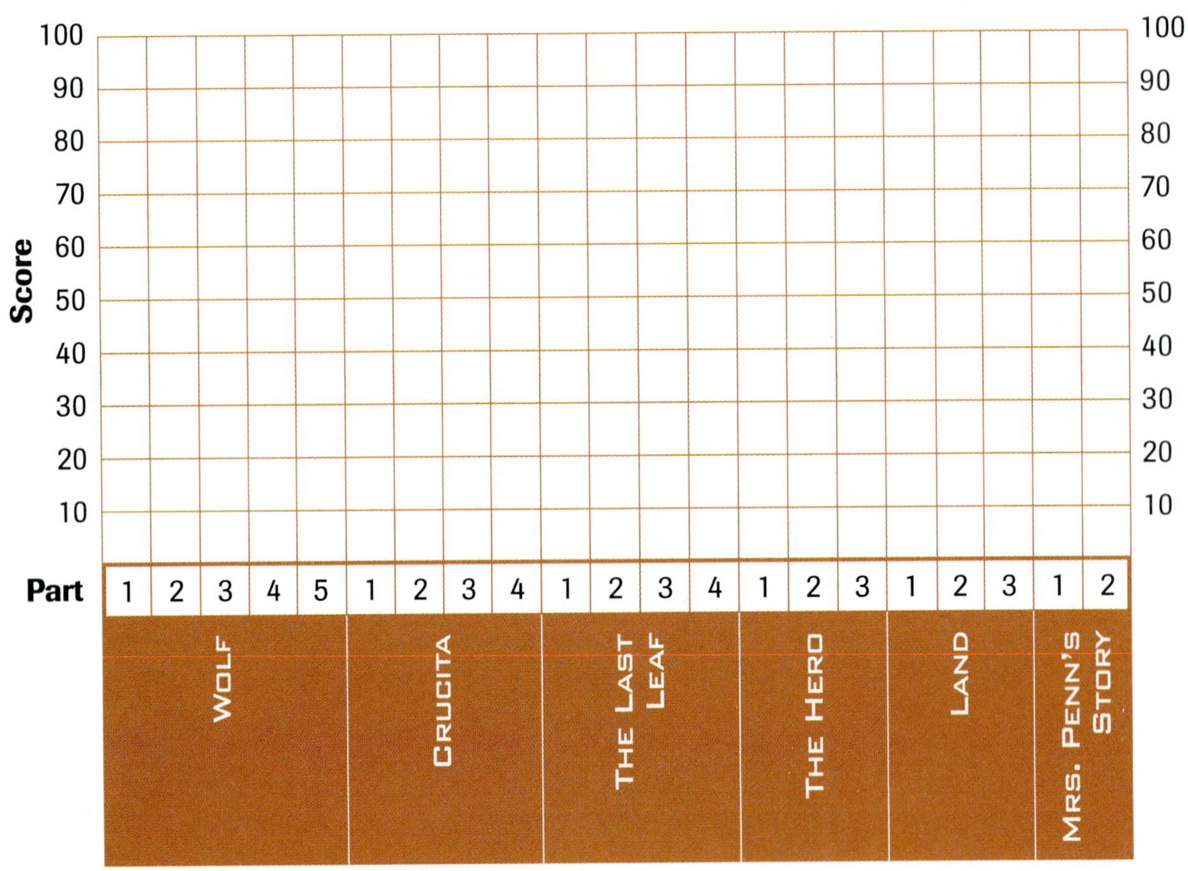